# REVEALING HEAVEN

## THE CHRISTIAN CASE FOR NEAR-DEATH EXPERIENCES

JOHN W. PRICE

HarperOne
*An Imprint of* HarperCollins*Publishers*

HarperOne

The quotation of Tess's account and interview by the Near-Death Experience Research Foundation are taken from their website, www.nderf.org, and printed with permission from Dr. and Mrs. Long.

Unless otherwise noted, all biblical quotations are taken from the New Revised Standard Version, copyright 1989, National Council of Churches of Christ in the U.S.A.



HarperCollins books may be purchased for educational, business, or sales promotional use. For information, please e-mail the Special Markets Department at SPsales@harpercollins.com.

HarperCollins website: http://www.harpercollins.com

HarperCollins®, ®, and HarperOne™ are trademarks of HarperCollins Publishers.

FIRST EDITION

Library of Congress Cataloging-in-Publication Data is available upon request.

ISBN 978–0–06–219771–9

13 14 15 16 17 RRD(H) 10 9 8 7 6 5 4 3 2 1

# CONTENTS

## PART II
# EXPLANATIONS

# PREFACE

When I became an Episcopal priest in 1965, I knew I would have to deal with death. I had no idea, however, that I would hear so many accounts from people who came back from it. Over the last forty years, I have listened to the stories of more than two hundred people who experienced life on the other side, and I have researched many more. This book analyzes those events and my reactions to them. There are dozens of books and compilations of near-death accounts by the people who had the experience. There is no need for me to add to that collection. Nor is there a need for me to explore the scientific aspects of this phenomenon. Several well-qualified medical doctors have already done this, particularly Raymond A. Moody Jr., Elisabeth Kübler-Ross, Melvin Morse, Pim van Lommel, John Audette, and Jeffrey Long, most of whom I reference and cite in the following pages.

I write strictly as a pastor, one who is deeply privileged to have heard so many accounts. As a clergyman, I am concerned that most people who have had the experience are reluctant to talk about it. This should not be the case. These stories should be shouted from the rooftops. The *spiritual* aspects of these accounts fascinate me. They follow so closely the understanding I have of the loving nature of God as shown in the person of Jesus of Nazareth in the New Testament.

If you want to know what heaven is like or what God has in store for us when we die, this is the book for you. Within these pages, I examine in full several near-death experiences. In doing so, I trace the similarities and patterns found in each account and highlight the pastoral and theological implications of these experiences. For far too long pastors, clergy, and lay Christians around the world have dismissed these experiences as meaningless flights of fancy that run counter to our faith. My argument is the exact opposite. I believe these experiences are central to our Christian faith. Each account verifies for the Christian community God's love and promise of eternal life in a literal heaven. As Christians, we should celebrate these near-death accounts as living testaments of this promise.

In addition to wanting to share these stories, I have other goals for this book. First, I want to comfort people who are curious, perhaps worried, about their eternal destiny. As a pastor, I get questions about this occasionally, when people are facing the reality of their own death. Is it a demise or a development? Final event or future unfolding? What about hell? People who are loving, as Jesus commanded, will find great news in these accounts. People who live lives of hate, anger, revenge, control, cruelty, and meanness toward others should read the distressing accounts carefully.

Second, I want to challenge believers and nonbelievers alike. We all need for those who have had their own near-death experience to share their stories with the world. (If you are a returnee who has experienced God's love face-to-face, don't be ashamed to spread the word!) And I want to encourage Christians, and members of the clergy in particular, to accept these experiences as gifts from God, as part of the gospel, and incorporate them and their insights into their ministries. We must communicate to people facing death the deeply comforting, faith-affirming facts of the near-death accounts as well as help those who have undergone a near-death experience grapple with this life-changing event.

Finally, I want to address those who feel that either their understanding of doctrine or what the Bible teaches forces them to reject these accounts of visits to heaven. I ask you to *listen* to the people who have interacted face-to-face with God or one of two kinds of spiritual beings, either one of light or one of darkness. Too many Christians discount these narratives because they contradict what they have been taught and thus believe about God. To a person, returnees tell us about the forgiving nature of God, regardless of a person's faith group, lifestyle, sexual preference, or lot in life. I challenge you to compare these insights to your own strongly held beliefs about God's judgmental view of humanity. I see a serious disconnect between what some faith groups teach and preach about God—for example, that he is angry, violent, and narrow—on the one hand, and what returnees tell us: that God is loving, accepting, and full of grace.

One person's near-death experience is that individual's own treasured event. But there are too many amazing similarities between these experiences for them to be mere coincidence. At the same time, there are also some interesting differences in these accounts, which give us even more intriguing insights into the will and nature of God. People with differing cultural or religious backgrounds and circumstances show us a broader spectrum of human existence and God's response to the varying situations. I see many important implications in what people have shared with me.

Based on my decades of experience in dealing personally and pastorally with many dozens of returnees, I am left with only one viable conclusion: near-death accounts are real. We need to accept them as such. Often a life change will occur—both for the one who tells it and the one who hears it. Such a major change of outlook on life happened to me.

This is not a new gospel. It is the same gospel: God loves us, forgives us, redeems us, and saves us for eternal life. We are still being offered "good news" from heaven, if we have ears to hear.

*The Rev. John W. Price*

# PART I

# DISCOVERY

# 1

# ALBERTO'S STORY

I do not have the typical background of a clergyman. Growing up, I was taught to respect the rational traditions of science and technology. All the men in our extended family were engineers, scientists, or technicians. Although I was raised in the Episcopal Church, even serving as an acolyte and singing in the choir, deep faith never came naturally to me. My family advised and prepared me for a life as an engineer. They wanted me to work in and perhaps later manage the highly successful engineering and manufacturing business my namesake, Uncle John, had run for decades. Like all his nephews, I worked summers at the plant. I was the only one who returned year after year. I discovered I was good at the engineering concepts, but realized this was not what I wanted to do with my life.

As a freshman at the University of Texas, I abandoned engineering and switched to history and psychology to prepare for ministry in the Episcopal Church. But although I became a pastor, I nonetheless remained as close to a rational materialist as a clergyman could. Despite my new career, I had no clear understanding of heaven, life's great mystery. Back then, I am now embarrassed to admit, I never fully believed in life after death.

In the middle of my seminary years, doctors discovered that my mother had lung cancer, and they kept her alive for six months. Every young child's dread is that his or her parents will die. At the time of my mother's death, I was studying at the Virginia Theological Seminary in Alexandria. The seminary community was an enormous help to me during the most difficult time I had faced to date.

But there was no *spirituality,* as I've come to understand it, in the comfort they gave me, nor in the classroom instruction. It would be another decade before the discussion of spirituality began. Back then, I wasn't even sure I would have understood the meaning of the word. If we had discussed spirituality, we might have drifted over into the nature of life after death, but "heaven" was only referred to obliquely. In our discussions, we were principally interested in social justice and the interpretation of scripture.

At one point, I tried in a term paper to discuss the concept of the love of God and the importance of it for life in the church. The professor gave me a "C" with the comment, "I do not get this 'love' business." The lesson I took home was not to experiment in an academic setting. I realized I would not be able to explore the issue until I had my own pulpit.

In my first two parish assignments as an assistant, I did not try to develop a different focus from what the senior pastor was preaching. I stayed with conventional themes in my sermons. In fact, I rarely preached about heaven during my early years as a priest. I was never fully comfortable with the subject. Thus, like many clergy today, I either didn't talk about it or would quickly change the subject to the importance of dealing with life in the here and now whenever it came up.

## TWO DISMISSED

On two separate occasions, members of my congregation tried to talk to me about their experiences with life after death. Right after I became rector/pastor of St. George's Episcopal Church in Austin, Texas, a woman named Betty confided to me that she had died and gone to heaven. I did not encourage her in the telling, so she dropped the subject. A few years later, during a parish exchange with the Church of England, a Londoner named Charles tried to tell me a similar story. I dismissed him as an English kook. During the last week of my stay, Charles gave me a copy of a typed book containing his account. I put it down and lost it in the confusion of my departure. I wish I had it now.

I dismissed both accounts largely because neither story fit neatly into my understanding of the pursuit of the Christian religion and faith. I didn't want to get off into a topic I considered just so much speculation. Return from heaven? Come on, let's get real. Don't turn religion into a joke or a ghost story.

It would only be a few more months before I realized the mistake I had made. My personal evolution started in May 1976, when I read *Life After Life,* Raymond A.

Moody's groundbreaking work about life after death.[1] In his book, Moody describes the experiences of 150 people who swear something happened to them while clinically dead. More than that, they *described* the events. Moody coined the term "near-death experience" (NDE). While reading it, I recognized that this was what both Betty and Charles had tried to describe to me. Perhaps, I distinctively remember thinking at the time, there's something to this.

## THEN I WAS STUNNED

The next month, I reported to the 49th Armored Division in Ft. Hood as Acting Division Chaplain with the Texas Army National Guard for my annual two-week training commitment. At the beginning of the second week, the chief of staff asked me to help a young Mexican American private I'll call Alberto. He had fractured his femur during a training exercise. Though Alberto had been medically cleared to return to San Antonio, his hometown, he had no way of getting there. His fellow unit members wanted the National Guard to take him home in a chopper, but the chief rightly denied their request. After some deliberation, I volunteered my driver to take Alberto 180 miles south in the colonel's new white Ford LTD. I would accompany them to secure the car.

We were not even out of Ft. Hood when he started to tell me about his experience. "I have something to tell you, Sir," he said.

> I'm not proud of myself when I was growing up. My friends and I were sniffing glue and paint when we were in elementary school, and doing badly in school. When I got into junior high, I was introduced to marijuana, and we started doing joints a lot. Then in high school, I got into the hard stuff and dropped out of school. I left home and went to California for the drug scene. I was really hooked.

I had no idea where Alberto was going with his story. A part of me wished he'd stop talking. Another part of me, however, understood I needed to hear him out. It didn't seem to me at the time that he was bragging about his exploits; rather, he regretted them. As he continued, I realized he had something important to share.

Alberto continued:

> Then one night at a drug party a guy gave me a pill and said, "Try this." I took it. It was the worst trip I'd ever had. It was painful, terrifying, and then suddenly I was at peace, with no pain. I felt like I was going through a tunnel, and there was this buzzing sound. Then there was this dude made of light, instead of flesh and bone, and he greeted me.

I flinched and cringed. I was stunned. I realized Alberto was describing the same kind of experience Moody wrote about in *Life After Life.* Had Alberto simply been trying to get my attention by making up a story he'd cribbed from Moody? I didn't think so—not then, and not now. His account was personal and quite detailed, unlike the depersonalized ones in Moody's book. As well, the book had only been on the shelves a few months and hadn't been serialized for a mass audience. It was hardly likely that Alberto would have read it. He wasn't making this up. This happened. His candor and sincerity and the matter-of-factness of his story convinced me. His experience, I realized, was as real as the highway in front of us.

The more Alberto spoke, the more I regretted doubting Betty and Charles. How could I have been so dismissive? I asked myself. How could I have been so arrogant to assume I knew better than they did about their experiences? I started to feel like a fraud. Here I was, an Episcopal priest, rector of a thriving parish, and I didn't believe in heaven? How could I counsel my parishioners about death or grief when I didn't believe the words coming out of my mouth?

I wanted to confess my past transgressions on this subject to Alberto. Before I could say a word, however, Alberto continued his remarkable story:

> Standing with the dude in white were my grandfather who'd died and some of my friends who'd died also. Then the dude in white reviewed my life with me, and I saw it like I was watching TV. I saw me with the glue and paint, then the marijuana and the hard stuff. He showed me I was throwing the gifts of God, the abilities and talents he'd given me, back in the face of God!
>
> Then I got to some sort of fence and was told it was not my time, and I woke up in my body. My buddies were standing over me, saying, "Hey, man, you scared us! Your skin turned gray. Your eyes were fixed. You weren't breathing." I got up and left them. I went back home, told my parents how sorry I was, got back in

high school, and graduated. I then joined the National Guard.

There in the car, I felt all my remaining doubts about life after death slowly fall away from my mind and its carefully schooled intellect. An overwhelming feeling of important discovery filled me. Alberto's story, following so closely on the heels of Moody's book, seemed to wash away all the doubts I had had about the afterlife. I immediately recognized the authenticity of Alberto's near-death experience. I knew there was no way he would have made it up and told it to me just to pass the time. Something life-changing had happened to him, an event that had to do with God, and if he was in a long car ride with a pastor, he was going to tell his story.

Could it be true? Could these near-death accounts be valid? I became convinced they were.

Within the accounts, I realized, lay facts that opened up to me the secrets of God's plan for us. Near-death experiences became a catalyst for spiritual development and transcendence, both for those who went through them and for people like me, the fortunate few allowed to hear their stories. Alberto's near-death experience changed him. He overcame his drug habit and turned his life around. His experience also changed me. For the first time, I began to understand there was far more to my vocation than I had ever thought. A whole new path was opening up for me. As Alberto spoke, I knew that I needed to share his story with as many people as possible who would listen.

But my road to Damascus continued past San Antonio. I still had a long way to go.

# 2

# MY STORY

Within the next couple of years, six other people told me about their near-death experiences. As yet, I was not actually seeking out these accounts. They found me. The most powerful story came from Frances, whose young daughter, Fran, came face-to-face with Jesus.

## FRAN'S STORY

A week after her baptism at age seven weeks, Fran developed a sinus infection, which constricted her breathing. One morning, as her mother nursed her, Fran suddenly went limp. Milk spilled from her mouth. Her eyes rolled back in her head. She stopped breathing, and her mother couldn't locate her daughter's pulse.

Frances and Fred, her husband, rushed Fran to the hospital, as Frances desperately tried to breathe air into her unconscious daughter. A team of doctors and nurses met them at the curb, whisked Fran away, and, after a few more frightful moments, resuscitated her. She was discharged from the hospital a few days later, happy and healthy as ever. Afterward, the family was more than happy to put the terrifying ordeal behind them.

And they did, until three years later when Frances drove past the hospital with Fran in the car.

"Look, Mommy," Fran said, pointing. "That's where Jesus brought me back to you."

Frances nearly drove off the road. She couldn't believe what she had just heard. She abruptly pulled the car over.

*"What did you say?"*

Fran was puzzled at her mother's reaction and said, "You know, Mommy. Jesus came and got me, but he brought me back to you there."

Frances had never told Fran about her trip to the emergency room. Nor did she ever talk to Fran about death or heaven—or God or Jesus, for that matter. There was no way Fran could have contrived this story. It actually happened, Frances realized. She never missed church after that.

Later, the grandmother of one of Fran's Sunday School classmates passed away. The teacher used the opportunity the next Sunday to talk about heaven and God's promise of eternal life. After the teacher finished her lesson, Fran raised her hand.

"Oh, yes, when you die," she told the class, "Jesus comes and gets you, but he brings you back if it's not your time."

## IT'S COMING TOGETHER

*If it's not your time.* Fran's words to her class brought to mind what Alberto told me during our trip to San Antonio: "It was not my time." As I continued to try to get a handle on Fran's and Alberto's stories, I returned to Moody's *Life After Life.* Although no two experiences are exactly alike, Moody reported that near-death experiences all generally proceed through several distinct movements:

- An out-of-body experience
- A sense of movement through a tunnel
- A great light
- An overwhelming feeling of love
- A reunion with deceased loved ones
- A sense of being in the most beautiful place, with the most beautiful music
- A review of one's life
- A brief period of instruction
- A border or point of no return
- Being told, "It is not your time"
- Waking up in one's own body

Later, after hearing different accounts, I would learn that the point when one is told "It's not your time" can occur at any time in the process. Fran and Alberto both reached a final point when Jesus told them they had to go back; it wasn't their time. No matter when it happens, though, I came to find out that this is a key element of many near-death experience stories, all of which unfold in remarkably consistent ways.

When I compared all the stories I heard with the

ones Moody wrote about in *Life After Life,* I realized there was a theological truth at the heart of all these stories: God has a plan for all of us, including a specific "time" for each of us to cross over to the continuation of our life in heaven. As a pastor, the truth came into focus: God loves and understands us. God forgives us and redeems us. God takes care of us, especially in our hour of greatest need. God is always present in our lives. We are a soul with a temporary body. Death is only a moment in the ongoing life of a consciousness, of a person, of a *soul*.

## KIRK'S STORY

I immediately put this realization to use by incorporating Alberto's, Fran's, and others' stories into my pastoral work. The first person I shared them with was Kirk, an elderly parishioner dying of cancer.

Like some people facing death, Kirk was terrified. He was distressed, angry, sobbing, and, because of a crude early form of chemotherapy, in a tremendous amount of pain. To help ease his mind, I decided to tell him about Alberto's and Fran's experiences. I started off slowly, still a little unsure about how he would react. I was concerned that Kirk would think I was crazy and then reject anything I had to say.

As I progressed through Alberto's story and then Fran's, however, he started to listen attentively to what I was saying. His eyes lit up, and he leaned toward me, as if he didn't want to miss a word. I knew I was starting to get through to him. I could see the signs of fear and anger slowly leave his face. He seemed to relax; his entire attitude changed. After a lengthy pause, in deep awe, he finally said, "I'm going to have to think about this."

I agreed to visit him the next afternoon. I understood the significance of my message. How often does a priest tell his parishioner that heaven is real, that God is just right there waiting for us to join him, that our "deceased" loved ones are just beyond God, waiting with a welcoming party? How often does a priest offer real accounts as proof of all this? I knew Kirk needed some time to let this realization sink in. After all, it took time for me to sort it all out, as it does for people who have had the experience themselves.

When I returned to the hospital the next afternoon, I wasn't sure what Kirk's reaction would be, whether, after thinking about the stories, he had embraced them or dismissed them completely. Of course I wanted Kirk to believe me, but I understood how big a leap of faith I was asking him to take. I approached his room with a fair amount of anxiety churning inside me. Before I reached the door, however, a nurse stopped me.

"*You!*" she said excitedly. "Aren't you the preacher who saw the man in this room yesterday afternoon?"

"Yes, I saw him," I said. "Is something wrong?"

"Wrong? No! He's different since you saw him! Before you saw him, he was very difficult, always complaining, sobbing, carrying on, making life difficult for the nurses, and disturbing the other patients with his wailing. Now his entire attitude is different. He's not complaining or carrying on. He's in there singing now. *What did you say to him?*"

As I explained what I had told him, her eyes glazed over and she walked away. It's okay, I thought, I was there less than a year ago.

*He's different since you saw him!*

Sure enough, when I entered Kirk's room, he was beaming with delight. He talked excitedly about what I'd told him. He said he wanted to know more. We visited for quite some time, going over the few accounts that had been told to me by then and the accounts in *Life After Life*. He asked me question after question about heaven and life after death. At the end of our conversation, he asked to receive Holy Communion. Because I didn't have my Communion kit with me, I consecrated some crackers and a glass of Welch's grape juice. To this day, our informal celebration of the Eucharist there in his hospital room remains one of the most profound religious experiences I've had as a pastor.

It was clear to me that Kirk knew that no matter what happened, God would take care of him. He had accepted in his heart God's invitation to unconditional and eternal love, with immediate acceptance into heaven after one's death. The word "Eucharist" comes from the Greek *eucharistia,* which means "thanksgiving." This was literally a thanksgiving for both of us. Kirk lived a few weeks more and was happy the whole time, telling me how much he was looking forward to his Great Adventure. That was only the second time I had witnessed such a stunning life change, a true conversion. The other was my own, when Alberto told me his account in 1976, a wonderful year for me.

This was a seminal period for me as a pastor. Through Alberto's and Fran's stories, I was able to help

Kirk and many more parishioners through their darkest hour. The near-death experiences allowed me to communicate what awaits us after we die—more effectively and articulately than any homily or sermon ever could. I felt incredibly fortunate to have heard these stories. I understood their inherent power. Just six months earlier, I wasn't sure I believed in such a thing as heaven. After hearing these first-person accounts from people who experienced something astounding after death, not only did I believe in heaven; I was now telling everyone I could about the details of arriving there. For the first time, I realized, I was in possession of a set of pastoral and spiritual tools with which to work. Others needed to hear about this.

## HOW THE CHURCH RESPONDS

Excited, I started to tell my fellow clergy about how near-death experiences had improved my pastoral work, while strengthening my own faith. Their reaction surprised me. A few were excited, but most dismissed these experiences. Some clergy even walked away when I brought up the subject.

One time, I went to the Episcopal seminary in Austin to visit with the professor of pastoral theology, a good friend, to tell him how the accounts helped console Kirk during his darkest hour. I felt this near-death phenomenon was important information to teach future members of the clergy in preparation for their pastoral work.

I ran into him on the sidewalk outside the classroom building. I told him my story. With him was another well-respected professor, important in the life of the seminary community.

"What's your take on all this?" I asked. They just shook their heads.

"No, it didn't happen," my friend said, as the other agreed. "There's no such thing as life after death. It's just race memory, or something like that. Hallucinations, probably."

"That's right," said the professor of systematic theology.

I was stunned. My expectations of sharing this great pastoral tool with future clergy were dashed. No such thing as life after death? I couldn't believe it. This, from two *seminary* professors?

"Well," I stammered, "what are we doing here, then?"

I thought for sure they would have some extensive insight into life after death, that my own previous doubts were mine alone, that these learned professors would certainly know the truth. Why didn't *they* believe in heaven? Why didn't they believe *me*? Why didn't they believe in this basic element of the *Christian faith*?

I understood that *redemption* is for this life, and *salvation* is for the next, eternal life; that we are saved for eternal life is certainly one of the principal teachings of Christianity. But these Christian clergymen believed there was no such thing as life after death.

I realized that I had just destroyed my reputation with the leading professors of the seminary community. But since they didn't believe in the central tenet of the Christian faith, it really didn't matter to me. I knew I was on the right track.

That's when I realized how much work I still needed to do to convince leaders of the church about the power of near-death experiences and the truth about heaven. Unfortunately, I'm sorry to write, it's been an uphill battle.

# 3

# IT'S IN THE BIBLE

Like any good pastor, I turned to the Bible for help. I needed to be able to substantiate my early conclusions. What I had come to understand from people's stunning and seemingly valid experiences should be reflected in the Holy Scriptures, I thought. What does the Bible have to say on the subject? What could I find that would shed light on this phenomenon?

I didn't remember coming across any specific statements on phenomena like near-death experiences in the scripture passages I had read in church or in my personal reading. What I discovered, though, was that I had read such passages earlier, but that I had brushed them aside because I didn't understand them. I had nothing to which I could relate these passages, and so I dismissed them. As I reread and studied now, however, they leaped out at me. I realized the statements supporting the validity of near-death experiences were there.

## 1 SAMUEL

Many people are shocked when they learn that in much of the Old Testament there is no teaching about life after death. Only later in Israel's history does the idea appear, and even then it is very unlike the Christian idea of heaven.

During the time between the prophet Samuel (near the end of the period of the judges) and the writing of the book of Daniel (second century BCE), there were two concepts of life after death that existed side by side. The earlier and more dominant view was that the body was buried in the ground and left alone for eternity; there was nothing more. (During New Testament times, the Sadducees, Jesus's frequent debate partners, were the ones who held this position; see Matthew 22:23; Mark 12:18; Luke 20:27.) I have spoken with a few rabbis who hold this position today. Obviously, there are some Christians who agree, such as the two seminary professors I consulted in 1977.

The second view, that there is some sort of existence after death, is seen in the biblical command to have nothing to do with people who consult the dead. Such a command presumes the idea that the dead were still alive in some way that would allow them to be summoned for communication. Moses expanded on the Ten Commandments with additional rules in Leviticus. There he said on behalf of the Lord, "Do not turn to mediums or wizards; do not seek them out, to be defiled by them: I am the Lord your God" (19:31). Deuteronomy instructs the Israelites not to "consult ghosts or spirits" or "seek oracles from the dead" (18:11).

In 1 Samuel 28, however, just before the rise of King David, we encounter the story of King Saul's interaction with one of these forbidden mediums—and the results are not favorable. The passage explains that Saul had indeed "expelled the mediums and wizards from the land" (v. 3), but Saul was about to encounter a much larger army of Philistines and was desperate for the kind of counsel he once received from the prophet Samuel, who was now deceased. We are told Saul prayed to the Lord, but "the Lord did not answer him" (v. 6).

Desperate, Saul tells one of his attendants, "Seek out for me a woman who is a medium, so I may go to her and inquire of her" (v. 7). He learns there is one in Endor nearby. Thus informed, Saul disguises himself and seeks out this medium. When he finds her, he asks her to "consult a spirit" (v. 8) for him. She responds,

> "Whom shall I bring up for you?" He answered, "Bring up Samuel for me." [12]When the woman saw Samuel, she cried out with a loud voice; and the woman said to Saul, "Why have you deceived me? You are Saul!" [13]The king said to her, "Have no fear; what do you see?" The woman said to Saul, "I see a divine being coming up out of the ground." [14]He said to her, "What is his appearance?" She said, "An old man is coming up; he is wrapped in a robe." So Saul knew that it was Samuel, and he bowed with his face to the ground, and did obeisance.
>
> 15 Then Samuel said to Saul, "Why have you disturbed me by bringing me up?" Saul answered, "I am in great distress, for the Philistines are warring against me, and God has turned away from me and answers me no more, either by prophets or by dreams; so I have summoned you to tell me what I should do." [16]Samuel

> said, "Why then do you ask me, since the Lord has turned from you and become your enemy? [17]The Lord has done to you just as he spoke by me; for the Lord has torn the kingdom out of your hand, and given it to your neighbor, David. [18]Because you did not obey the voice of the Lord, and did not carry out his fierce wrath against Amalek, therefore the Lord has done this thing to you today. [19]Moreover, the Lord will give Israel along with you into the hands of the Philistines; and tomorrow you and your sons shall be with me; the Lord will also give the army of Israel into the hands of the Philistines." (28:11–19)

Of this second view, death as a kind of sleep that should not be disturbed, Jaime Clark-Soles says in *Death and the Afterlife in the New Testament:*

> Samuel was awakened from his death-sleep by the medium. He communicated with Saul. This was the one concept of life after death at this point in Israel: sleep, from which one can be temporarily awakened to communicate. Archaeological evidence shows food and other offerings have been found in ancient Jewish burials. However, it is not clear whether this is for their

use in the next life or simply an offering of esteem for the deceased by grieving loved ones.[1]

## DANIEL

As I continued to search, the next biblical description of the afterlife I found was in the final chapter of Daniel. A little background information is necessary to understand the setting. Daniel was written in the second century BCE, after Alexander the Great had conquered the Middle East in 332. After Alexander's death in 323 BCE, his generals fought over portions of his empire. Judea eventually came under the control of the Seleucids in 198 BCE. During this era, Seleucid leaders erected an altar to Zeus in the Temple in Jerusalem. Jews believed the Holy of Holies, the Temple's most sacred part, was the location of God's throne. By putting an altar to a Greek god in the Temple, the Greeks had desecrated the Temple and shamed and humiliated the conquered Jews.[2]

The author of Daniel composed the book to give hope to the subjugated Israelites. He wanted to convey to his beleaguered fellow Jews that God was with them even under the devastating rule of the pagan Seleucid Greeks. Suppression, murder of dissidents, and the insertion of Greek polytheistic images and rites into Jewish religious sites made for an intolerable cultural situation. In one historical example after another, this sort of frustration produces apocalyptic literature, which promises better times to come. Set in a prophetic style with examples of deliveries from intolerable situations, it offers a message that is very soothing to the victims of current oppression.

"Apocalypse" comes from *apokalypsis,* the Greek word for "revelation." Many people love the hint of secret knowledge perhaps revealed by an angel who promises—prophesies—a victorious conclusion to current strife. It sells books. Later readers, unaware of the circumstances under which the apocalypse was written, often take the symbolism in very different directions than was intended. An example is when some Protestants cast the pope as the "beast" with "the number 666" in the book of Revelation (13:18), when in fact the original reference was to the Roman emperor Nero.

Many Jews were killed during Seleucid rule when a harsh king, Antiochus IV, came to power in 175 BCE. Because any writings critical of this king would have brought down his wrath, the author of Daniel ostensibly wrote about Nebuchadnezzar, a Babylonian emperor who conquered Jerusalem in 586 BCE, four centuries earlier. Most contemporary Jews, however, recognized in the author's story the occupying Seleucid forces. So the author of Daniel consoles his readers with the promise of future glory.

The description of an afterlife in Daniel is sparse:

> At that time Michael, the great prince, the protector of your people, shall arise. There shall be a time of anguish, such as has never occurred since nations first came into existence. But at that time your people shall be delivered, everyone who is found written in the book. [2]Many of those who sleep in the dust of the earth shall awake, some to everlasting life, and some to shame and everlasting contempt. [3]Those who are wise shall shine like the brightness of the sky, and those who lead many to righteousness, like the stars for ever and ever. (12:1–3)

For the first time in the scriptures we read that there will be life after death. Those whose names are "found written in the book" will "awake" to "everlasting life."

God will remember who deserved everlasting life and who will be held in shame and everlasting contempt. "At that time" seems to indicate that the awakening will happen at some future date. Notice the words "heaven" and "hell" are not used.

Daniel offered two levels of comfort to the Jews of the day. On one level, this was simply an apocalyptic reference to a time when the Greeks would no longer be occupying the land and harassing the Jews. Apocalyptic literature is written to give hope to the oppressed. At "that time" of delivery, the faithful would live in peace and the others in shame and contempt. Consider the situation in France after the German forces were driven out in 1944. Women who had taken up with the Germans had their heads shaved as a mark of their shame. The collaborating men had their trousers removed and both were paraded in contempt before hooting and deriding Parisians. The Jews' oppressors would experience similar "everlasting contempt."

On a second level, this is the only Old Testament description of "everlasting life." It is cast as a reality within the reach of the righteous, though at some later, unspecified date. At death, the bodies go to Sheol, literally "the pit," where spirits or shades (Hebrew *rephaim*) await a lifting from the graves to go to judgment at some unspecified time. This apocalyptic prophecy by the author of Daniel added the new element to the Bible of the restored actual bodies being raised from the grave for judgment and final assignment later. Many Christians today still hold to this belief.

## 1 CORINTHIANS

My own beliefs about an afterlife prior to reading Moody's book and hearing Alberto's account were vague. I didn't know what to believe. Nothing after death? Bodies waiting in graves for the Second Coming? An instant arrival in heaven? Because I was unsure about what to think, for many years I concentrated on the quality of life we have here and now. I was committed to helping people live according to Jesus's commandment, "Love one another as I have loved you" (John 15:12), and his summary of the law, "You shall love the Lord your God with all your heart, and with all your soul, and with all your mind . . . [and] your neighbor as yourself" (Matthew 22:37–39). I felt that was all I was capable of doing. This, to me, was the Christian life.

I avoided any attempt to define what happens after the bodily functions cease. I trusted in God for whatever might follow death. I had enough to deal with without getting into speculation about life after death. Concentrating on living a life of love worked well in helping a congregation function productively. Then in the space of six months I quietly ignored a man who tried to tell me about his near-death experience, I read Moody's *Life After Life,* and I heard Private Alberto's stunning experience and the impact it had on his life. As you have heard, this opened my mind, many doors, and a new path of ministry.

I realized that the concepts found in 1 Samuel and Daniel—that we go into a sleeping state in a grave awaiting the return of the Messiah—are contradicted by the near-death accounts. The Sadducees' denial of any life after death is also put to rest, pun intended.

Those dating the various books of the New Testament believe Paul's letters to the Corinthians were written before the Gospels. They contain the first written record of what Christians believe about the afterlife, so I will explore Paul's letters first.

In the New Testament, Paul advances the idea of a literal heaven:

> But someone will ask, "How are the dead raised? With what kind of body do they come?" [36]Fool! What you sow does not come to life unless it dies. [37]And as for what you sow, you do not sow the body that is to be, but a bare seed, perhaps of wheat or of some other grain. [38]But God gives it a body as he has chosen, and to each kind of seed its own body. . . .
>
> 42 So it is with the resurrection of the dead. What is sown is perishable, what is raised is imperishable. [43]It is sown in dishonor, it is raised in glory. It is sown in weakness, it is raised in power. [44]It is sown a physical body, it is raised a spiritual body. If there is a physical body, there is also a spiritual body. . . .
>
> 50 What I am saying, brothers and sisters, is this: flesh and blood cannot inherit the kingdom of God, nor does the perishable inherit the imperishable. [51]Listen, I will tell you a mystery! We will not all die, but we will all be changed, [52]in a moment, in the twinkling of an eye, at the last trumpet. For the trumpet will sound, and the dead will be raised imperishable, and we will be changed. (1 Corinthians 15:35–52)

This concept of a "spiritual body" is a new introduction into the Bible's various concepts of the existence and nature of life after death. It says that the Sadducees were wrong; there is life after death. Paul's description contrasts markedly with Daniel's of sleeping in the grave until the Messiah comes. The transition from mortal body to a spiritual body takes place "in a moment, in the twinkling of an eye," not as some distant historical event or Daniel's end time.

Like the author of Daniel, Paul seems to suggest here that the changing to a spiritual body will come at some "last trumpet." Some take this to mean the change will happen at the Second Coming of Jesus. However, because Paul here refers to this as an instant, a moment ("the twinkling of an eye"), it could also be the moment of individual death. The "last trumpet" could sound for each person individually, not at some very last time for all deceased together.

My interpretation of Paul's "trumpet" sounding is that it happens the way the many returnees relate, in "the twinkling of an eye," that is, at the moment of death. At death we assume our spiritual body. As will become evident, Paul and other New Testament writers did not agree with the understanding of the "last trumpet" as the Second Coming. As we will see, his personal journey to the "third heaven" did not wait until the end time.

So my basic understanding of this passage *switched* as I realized that those who had a near-death experience testified to a very different "trumpet" moment: not at the Second Coming, but at the instant of death. The vagueness I had earlier felt about the death process was disappearing, melting away.

## THE GOSPEL OF LUKE

Most scholars agree that Paul's letters to the Corinthians were written in 55–56 CE. The date for Luke's Gospel is a few years *later*: between 59 and the 80s, depending on which scholar's dates you accept.[3]

It is significant that Paul's letters to the Corinthians were written before Luke's Gospel. His is the only Gospel to include the following parable about the rich man and the beggar Lazarus. They both died, but went in different directions after death; Lazarus "was carried away by the angels to be with Abraham," and the rich man, who ignored Lazarus's plight, went to "Hades":

> There was a rich man who was dressed in purple and fine linen and who feasted sumptuously every day.

[20]And at his gate lay a poor man named Lazarus, covered with sores, [21]who longed to satisfy his hunger with what fell from the rich man's table; even the dogs would come and lick his sores. [22]The poor man died and was carried away by the angels to be with Abraham. The rich man also died and was buried. [23]In Hades, where he was being tormented, he looked up and saw Abraham far away with Lazarus by his side. [24]He called out, "Father Abraham, have mercy on me, and send Lazarus to dip the tip of his finger in water and cool my tongue; for I am in agony in these flames." [25]But Abraham said, "Child, remember that during your lifetime you received your good things, and Lazarus in like manner evil things; but now he is comforted here, and you are in agony. [26]Besides all this, between you and us a great chasm has been fixed, so that those who might want to pass from here to you cannot do so, and no one can cross from there to us." [27]He said, "Then, father, I beg you to send him to my father's house—[28]for I have five brothers—that he may warn them, so that they will not also come into this place of torment." [29]Abraham replied, "They have Moses and the prophets; they should listen to them." [30]He said, "No, father Abraham; but if someone goes to them

> from the dead, they will repent." [31]He said to him, "If they do not listen to Moses and the prophets, neither will they be convinced even if someone rises from the dead." (16:19–31)

Some maintain that the description in Daniel "at that time your people shall be delivered" foreshadows the Second Coming of Christ. This is later prophesied in Luke's book of the Acts of the Apostles: "This Jesus, who has been taken up from you into heaven, will come in the same way as you saw him go into heaven" (1:11). However, in Luke's Gospel, Jesus tells one of the thieves crucified along with him, "Today you will be with me in Paradise" (23:43). There is no reference to Jesus having to return before the thief can be raised from the grave. So too in the parable above, we witness people in a version of a hell and a heaven, but they are there well before the end of time—in fact, they are there at a time when the rich man had five living brothers still on earth. This is different from the comments in Daniel. I am inclined to take Jesus's response to the thief and this parable as more authoritative than the description found in Daniel. As well, Jesus's promise to the thief is in keeping with the near-death accounts.

In the parable about the rich man and Lazarus, Luke does two things for the first time in the Gospels. First, as Paul did in 1 Corinthians 15, Luke reveals to us the immediacy of conscious life continuing after the moment of death. Second, Luke confirms the perception of the different realms after death described in Daniel ("everlasting life" versus "shame and contempt").

I was excited to put together the accounts of Alberto, Fran, and others as they came into my life, and now I realized how bold Paul's statement was regarding our transformation after death. He was the first biblical author to reveal that what happens in the afterlife, according to Christianity, aligns with what is revealed by near-death accounts, that upon death we are immediately transformed and brought into heaven.

Although we read accounts in the Bible of people who died and then were brought back to life—Lazarus of Bethany (John 11), the son of the widow of Nain (Luke 7:11–17), the son of the widow of Zarephath (1 Kings 17:17–24)—there isn't a word about their personal experience of the event. Perhaps they, like those with more current accounts before Moody's book, were surrounded by too many people who doubted the veracity of the phenomenon.

We all die. This much hasn't changed since Paul first corresponded with the Corinthians. But at the time of our death, Paul promises, we will be "raised imperishable" in the presence of God in heaven. I had always taken this statement as apocalyptic prophesy. I never took it seriously, if I thought about it at all.

## 2 CORINTHIANS

People in Corinth must have read Paul's first letter and challenged how he knew what heaven was like, because he returns to their question later in his second letter. He writes of a person becoming a "spiritual body" (*soma pneumatikon*) at death:

> So we are always confident; even though we know that while we are at home in the body we are away from
> the Lord—7for we walk by faith, not by sight. 8Yes, we
> do have confidence, and we would rather be away from
> the body and at home with the Lord. 9So whether we
> are at home or away, we make it our aim to please him.
> 10For all of us must appear before the judgment seat
> of Christ, so that each may receive recompense for

> what has been done in the body, whether good or evil. (2 Corinthians 5:6–10)

To answer the question of how he knows, Paul writes:

> [2]I know a man in Christ who fourteen years ago was
> caught up to the third heaven. Whether it was in the
> body or out of the body I do not know—God knows.
> [3]And I know that this man—whether in the body or
> apart from the body I do not know, but God knows—
> [4]was caught up to paradise and heard inexpressible
> things, things that no one is permitted to tell. (2 Corinthians 12:2–4, NIV)

*I know a man in Christ who fourteen years ago was caught up to the third heaven.* When I reread this passage after reading Moody and hearing Alberto, my eyebrows went up, my eyes opened wide, and so did my mouth. I gasped. Was Paul writing what I thought he was writing? Based on my experiences with Alberto and Fran, it certainly sounded as if Paul was describing a near-death experience. I read the passage over and over again.

*I know a man in Christ who . . .* Suddenly I remembered something from my seminary classes. I was taught that a few biblical authors used the third person to communicate something that had happened to them. In his Gospel, for instance, Mark describes an unnamed young man wearing only a linen cloth who was watching the betrayal and arrest of Jesus. One of the officers grabbed at "a certain young man" and caught only the cloth, which ripped away, and the young man ran away naked. Here Mark implies, "This was me. I was there for the whole thing. I saw it happen." In a commentary, New Testament scholar Frederick C. Grant agrees with this autobiographical interpretation of Mark's comment, adding that it was "the artist's signature in the corner of the painting."[4]

Four times in his Gospel, John mentions "the disciple whom Jesus loved" without naming him (13:23; 19:26; 21:7; 21:20). This implies it was John himself. Why else would this phrasing be used only in the Gospel of John? If we interpret Mark's and John's statements as autobiographical, then it appears that what Paul is telling the Corinthians about is something that happened to him. This is how he knows spiritual bodies feel "at home" after death. This corresponds exactly to how people who have had a near-death experience describe their feelings.

But what exactly did Paul mean when he wrote that

he was "caught up to the third heaven"? New Testament scholar Donald Guthrie explains this as one of Paul's three "visions": "This is a Jewish expression meaning to be actually in the presence of God."[5] Another Bible scholar explains Paul's description as that of one of the "abundant experiences of ecstasy which have been granted to [Paul], . . . [an] extraordinary vision and audition of the third, i.e., highest heaven."[6] There is no idea in these commentaries that it was a near-death experience, since there is no internal evidence in the document to make this conclusion. (And what scholar would be eager to make this bold claim in light of scholarly attitudes toward near-death experiences in general?) But it is a well-attested conclusion of many scholars that Paul was indirectly relating his own experience, but was uncomfortable doing so directly. (Just as many people are reluctant to talk about their near-death experiences today.)

I continued reading, hungry for more. Paul says we must all appear "before the judgment seat of Christ, that each one may receive what is due him for the things done while in the body, whether good or bad." (2 Corinthians 5:10, NIV). I immediately thought about what Alberto told me:

> Then the dude in white reviewed my life with me, and I saw it like I was watching TV. I saw me with the glue and paint, then the marijuana and the hard stuff. He showed me I was throwing the gifts of God, the abilities and talents he'd given me, back in the face of God!

This is exactly as Paul described it in his second letter to the Corinthians. At some point after the moment of one's death, God reviews in full a person's life, just as Alberto had said. Later, I would realize this is a common occurrence in almost every near-death experience, but right then I was stunned by the similarities between Paul's description of the events after death and Alberto's.

Paul's comments on life after death in his letters to the church in Corinth were ignored in my seminary instruction; biblical commentaries explained them away as an ecstatic vision. Yet here was yet another link to the revelations from the near-death insights. If I believed in near-death experiences before my investigation, I was now an ardent supporter, not only of the reality of their existence, but also of their theological and multiple biblical roots, which I had previously glossed over. Throughout history, people have sometimes come face-to-face with God, caught up "to the third heaven" and returned. As far as I was concerned this was the answer to one of the mysteries of life: death. I know the source of our hope and faith. When we die, God awaits our arrival, lovingly:

> Those who are wise shall shine like the brightness of the sky, and those who lead many to righteousness, like the stars forever and ever. (Daniel 12:3)

Here is what I knew. The phenomenon known popularly as the near-death experience is one in which a person's body dies. The soul departs, continues on a journey, and has certain experiences. These steps are common to the majority of the returnees' experiences. The individuals return after learning it was not their "time to die," which has serious implications for the Christian faith. Medical doctors writing about this phenomenon have stated they cannot make any judgments about the meaning of such experiences; they can only describe them. They declare that the sheer number and consistency of these accounts indicate they are real. The thousands of accounts are too consistent to be seriously labeled "anecdotal" and therefore of questionable validity and meaning.

Based on my knowledge of these accounts and my theological and biblical explorations, I realized that near-death experiences were valid, real, and authentic. They teach us a lot. There are solid theological, religious, spiritual, ethical, and pastoral lessons to be learned from them and used to aid the lives of all humanity.

This is the Christian case for near-death experiences. There is more.

# 4

# A HISTORY OF NEAR-DEATH EXPERIENCES

I was consumed by the accounts of near-death experiences, but my rational mind still wanted to take over. It wanted to make sense of this phenomenon. So I started reading as much about near-death experiences as I could.

## EARLY ACCOUNTS

The earliest recorded description of a near-death experience I could find dates from about 380–360 BCE. It is found in Book 10 of Plato's *Republic*, referred to derogatorily by some as the "Myth of Er." Plato recounts the story of Er, a Pamphylian warrior who died in battle. He woke up on the funeral pyre with his compatriots, his body miraculously preserved. After coming to, he related to his countrymen what he saw in the other world. He traveled to a mysterious region with two openings side by side in the earth, two openings in the heavens, and judges standing in between. After each judgment, he recounted, the just passed to the right, then continued upward through heaven, while the unjust were forced left, then continued downward to a different place. Note the similarity with the statements in the book of Daniel: "Many of those who sleep in the dust of the earth shall awake, some to everlasting life, and some to shame and everlasting contempt" (12:2) When Er drew near the divide, the judges told him he would serve as their messenger. They ordered him to tell others about this other world. They charged him to give ear and to observe everything in the place.

Er described the righteous souls of Orpheus, Thamyras, Ajax, Agamemnon, Atalanta, Epeus, Thersites, and Odysseus selecting their new lives. "The choice of the souls," Er writes, "was in most cases based on their experience of a previous life." After the eight souls chose, each one was led to the daughters of Necessity, Lachesis, Clotho, and Atropos—the Three Fates—whose spindle wove for each warrior a new destiny. The souls journeyed to the Plain of Oblivion and drank at the River of Forgetfulness, then fell asleep before ascending upward to their new birth like shooting stars. Er was not allowed to drink of the water, and he returned to his body on the funeral pyre.

Interestingly, Er was told to observe everything and tell about it. Paul was told things he said were inexpressible, "things that no one is permitted to tell." Some of the returnees with whom I've visited said they were taken off to the side by angels who taught them amazing things they simply can't remember. It is as though the angels were then told it was not this person's time and the memory of what was taught was erased. There is no mention that they were not *permitted* to tell; it is that they *cannot.* Many returnees say they cannot adequately express much of the experience in a *human* language.

Similar accounts of near-death experiences are found in traditional folklore throughout Europe, the Middle East, Africa, India, Asia, and indigenous cultures in North and South America. The Egyptian *Book of the Dead* and the Tibetan *Book of the Dead* are just two of the most popular ancient texts that contain accounts of near-death experiences from other cultures. Indeed, near-death experiences aren't limited to a particular race, gender, social class, age group, or *faith group*. They are, without question, universal experiences.

## CARL JUNG

In his autobiography, *Memories, Dreams, and Reflections,* Carl Jung, the great early twentieth-century psychiatrist, wrote about his own near-death experience in 1944:

> As I approached the temple I had the certainty that I was about to enter an illuminated room and would meet there all those people to whom I belong in reality. There I would at last understand—this too was a certainty—what historical nexus I or my life fitted into. I would know what had been before me, why I had come into being, and where my life was flow-

> ing. My life as I lived it had often seemed to me like a story that has no beginning and end. I had the feeling that I was a historical fragment, an excerpt for which the preceding and succeeding text was missing. My life seemed to have been snipped out of a long chain of events, and many questions had remained unanswered. Why had it taken this course? Why had I brought these particular assumptions with me? What had I made of them? What will follow? I felt sure that I would receive an answer to all the questions as soon as I entered the rock temple. There I would meet the people who knew the answer to my question about what had been before and what would come after.[1]

Later, during an interview with the BBC, a reporter asked Jung if he believed in God. "No," Jung replied, "I *know* God."

Although I was familiar with Jung's quote and was greatly encouraged by the "Myth of Er" and both versions of the *Book of the Dead,* what I discovered in the United States in the late 1970s and early 1980s really excited me and helped me realize the true value—and growing presence—of near-death experiences.

## LATE TWENTIETH-CENTURY DEVELOPMENTS

In 1975, John Audette, a sociologist interested in near-death experiences because of Elisabeth Kübler-Ross's recent writings on the subject, introduced Moody and Kübler-Ross to each other prior to the publication of *Life After Life.* As a result of the meeting, Kübler-Ross wrote the foreword to his book. She had personally experienced the rejection of colleagues following her own work and congratulated Moody for having the courage to publish his findings. She was a courageous woman herself, as she continued to write and lecture on near-death experiences despite vocal opposition from physicians and clergy.

These three, joined by social psychologist Kenneth Ring, Ph.D., clinical psychologist Bruce Greyson, M.D., and Michael Sabom, M.D., began the whole near-death experience revolution in America. Pim van Lommel, M.D., later started the International Association for Near-Death Studies in Holland. Each contributed greatly to the research and growing number of publications on the subject. Greyson edited the *Journal of Near-Death Studies* for the International Association for Near-Death Studies (IANDS) for many years and enriched the understandings of the phenomenon in mainstream science, religion, and popular culture. The journal continues to this day.

In 1981, Ring took over as director of IANDS. A professor of psychology and researcher at the University of Connecticut, Ring visited hospitals around Hartford, where he interviewed patients who had been either very close to physical death or pronounced clinically dead by medical staff. He asked these patients if they remembered anything during this time. He found, to my amazement, that roughly one-third of these patients underwent some kind of transcendental experience.[2]

That same year, just six years after the publication of *Life After Life,* the influential Gallup organization found that 15 percent of American adults had what its official pollster, George Gallup, called "verge-of-death experiences." In the survey, people described their experiences variously as "an overwhelming sense of peace and painlessness," "a fast review . . . of one's life," and an "out-of-body sensation." These included a distinct "perception of a tunnel" and an "acute visual perception of surroundings and events."[3] These descriptions were not provided as multiple-choice options, but were written in the respondents' own hand. Despite the different terms—"verge-of-death experience" versus "near-death experience"—the descriptions were the same.

Gallup's numbers astounded me. As a percentage, more living people had had a near-death experience by 1981 than the total attendance at all Major League Baseball games in that year,[4] which seemed hard to believe. Still, even if only one-tenth of that number were the case, that would mean millions of Americans had had a near-death experience. And this was just the United States. What about Latin America, Europe, Asia, Africa? I would expect that countries with good emergency-response teams would report large numbers of resuscitations as well.

As the numbers steadily climbed, my reaction was puzzlement. How astonishing! Why have returnees been so silent about their experiences?

As I visited with more and more returnees, several possible reasons for the reluctance occurred to me. They had had the most precious experience of their lives and didn't want it denigrated by insensitive people. They were afraid of being thought *weird, crazy,* or *strange.* They kept quiet because no minister or physician had brought up the subject following their clinical death. Some clergy rejected their accounts. I rejected accounts, twice. Some were urged by the first person they told, such as their mother or, in one instance, a nun, never to bring it up again. I understood these feelings. I had treated the first two returnees I spoke to with suspicion and applied those very labels.

Still, as I reflected on the growing number of near-death experiences, I realized these weren't fringe experiences. They were quickly becoming the norm, very much in line with my unofficial tally in Austin, where I continued to hear more accounts from members of my own congregation. None affected me more than Ella's account.

## ELLA'S STORY

In 1968, I was elected rector of St. George's Episcopal Church, a struggling parish in Austin. Since its founding eighteen years earlier, the church had burned through six priests, all of whom had been run off by three warring factions within the parish who cared more about petty victories and gamesmanship than building a supportive community. When I arrived, I preached repeatedly about the love of God and Jesus's

Great Commandment for us to love one another, just as he had. I repeatedly stressed Jesus's message of forgiveness and reconciliation and praying for our enemies. Eventually, my message resonated with the congregation, and it slowly settled down, one member at a time.

Except for one. Though she kept quiet for a couple of years, she had had enough of my positive messages of God's love. Just as she had done with my predecessors, she tried to force me out. But I wouldn't have it. I'd worked too hard to bring this congregation together. I wasn't about to let her tear it or my career apart. When she threatened to leave the church, I didn't beg her to stay. When she threatened to take people with her, I offered her the parish directory. She left, taking, as promised, five families with her.

The congregation and I slowly breathed a nervous sigh of relief. The fighting was finally over. Parish life increased in quality and quantity as a result. The congregation began to grow, the giving and subsequent budget leaped ahead, and programs exploded. Parish life became wonderful. Amazingly, some eight years later, the woman returned with four of the five families. This time they were more open, loving, and cooperative! It was a really great development in the life of the parish. A true redemption had occurred.

Within three months, however, one of the returning women, Ella, was diagnosed with terminal cancer. I helped her family set up a hospice in their home after it was obvious there was nothing more the hospital could do. One Sunday afternoon, her husband called me at home. "Please come," he said, rather nervously.

When I walked in the door of their home, everyone looked nervous, and Ella, too weak to speak, looked at me with great awe.

"What is going on?" I asked.

The nurse, visibly shaken, explained that before Ed phoned me, she noticed Ella hadn't moved in a long time. Tentatively, she listened with her stethoscope for a pulse or for any breathing. She found none. She lifted back the patient's eyelids, observed that the pupils were restricted and fixed, and then pricked her arm with a needle. Seeing no response, she turned to the husband and said, "Ella's gone."

Ella's husband and daughter went to the bedside and wept. After a while he turned to the telephone and started dialing my home number. During the old rotary-dial process, the nurse let out a stunned gasp.

Ed turned and saw Ella moving her head and looking around the room, quite alive. He returned to his dialing. I answered, and he said, "Please come."

Two days later, the daughter was feeding her mother when Ella said, "John Price is right. God does want us to pray for our enemies and not work against them." Her daughter, not understanding, asked what her mother meant. Ella said:

> I was lying here in bed when Jesus came through the ceiling, held his hands down to me, and I lifted my hands to him. He lifted me up through the ceiling. I saw my [dead] grandparents, brother, and other friends who had died; it was so beautiful. Then I went through a review of my life. In it, I knew how God disapproved of what I did to the clergy and others in the parish. Then I was hearing John Price's sermons over again, and God told me, "John Price is right, God does want us to pray for our enemies and not to work against them."

This was one of the points I had repeatedly made in my sermons. Ella lived another week, and in that time the word got out quickly that something absolutely stunning had happened. Over a few days, nearly two dozen women came to visit her. She told them the same story of her near-death experience. Later that week, she died, surrounded by her family.

I thought of Er, from Plato's *Republic,* who was sent back to tell his story. Was this why Ella was sent back? If so, she didn't say, but she lived out her purpose quite well.

After her funeral, the women sat down with me to discuss Ella's experience. "Do you believe her?" they asked. I told them about Alberto and Fran. I also told them everything I knew about the near-death phenomenon. Ella, I stressed, was only one of many returnees.

I felt as though we were walking on holy ground. A miracle had happened to Ella and, through her, to the church. The once warring factions were back in the fold, but this time they were peaceful, docile, and, more important, loving. Within that now warm and loving congregation, a double miracle had occurred. There was reconciliation in God's love and the return of one of the principals from the very presence of God. All proclaimed that the message of God's love as a way to live was powerfully right. Word got out rapidly in the parish, and for years afterward people responded enthusiastically to anything I suggested! God had endorsed me, the sentiment went, and this repentant, returned, redeemed woman had relayed the endorsement!

A paradigm shift had occurred in that congregation that love was the way to live in harmony. This realization was made all the more emphatic with a second paradigm shift that someone could return from death and talk about the lessons learned relative to love. Those were stunning times in the 1970s and 1980s. Minds were opened, new concepts about life and death emerged, spirituality fairly exploded. I completed twenty years as rector of that parish, longer than all my predecessors put together. We accomplished great things together. And my successor surpassed my record for length of service, I'm very happy to say.

# 5

# MY STORY CONTINUED

At this point in my ministry, I was now open and eager to pay attention to the deeply moving accounts of people's lives continuing past the moment of death and their returning to tell such consistent descriptions of the events. They came along with more regularity.

What now? These accounts that kept on coming into my life opened me to even more possibilities. Spirituality had been an unknown element in the congregations I had attended, my seminary education, and my religious life. The hotly debated issues in the church in the 1950s and 1960s were civil rights, church rituals, and liturgical reform. As well, charges of Communism in the National Council of Churches and the validity of the Revised Standard Version of the Bible versus the "official" King James Version fueled insidious arguments within the church. These dominated all religious discussions. Any attempt to address spirituality was perceived as lame and unworthy. How could we abandon the highly important "real" issues? Spirituality had little importance. How sad, I now reflect. No one I knew in those days had enough information about spirituality for a proper discussion.

It didn't get any better when I graduated from the seminary in 1964 and went to serve as an assistant in a couple of parishes. But I felt something was missing. I just didn't know what it was, rather like the rich young man who asked Jesus what else he could *do* to inherit eternal life. The young man was asking the wrong question. The real question is, what must I *be?* The answer I realized from the near-death accounts is that God gives eternal life to us out of his love. Spirituality, as I've since come to understand it, is seeking a close relationship with God in our daily lives. The church has passed down a variety of means for pursuing an exhilarating spiritual life, such as various styles of prayer and meditation, journaling, reading the writings from earlier times when spirituality was widely lived, all of which assist in deepening one's relationship with God. I understand this now, but I had no such grasp of spirituality back then.

## SPIRITUAL RENEWAL

Fortunately, events were unfolding that would enable the wider practice of spiritual growth for me. In 1958, Cardinal Angelo Giuseppe Roncalli was elected pope of the Roman Catholic Church. During his brief papacy as John XXIII, he started a spiritual revolution in the Roman Catholic Church, which eventually spilled over in various forms into the Anglican Communion and Lutheran churches, then to Presbyterian and Methodist churches. A renewal movement swept through churches previously concerned only with relatively secular issues by comparison. These external events dovetailed with my own personal experiences with Moody's book and Private Alberto and little Fran. I don't know if the same events came together for others as they did for me, but I became a leader in some of the programs of the spiritual renewal movement in the Episcopal diocese of Texas.

## IMPROVED MEDICAL CARE

Another sweeping change was developing in medical care in cities across the country in the 1960s. Previously, ambulances were merely plain hearse-type vehicles without trained emergency medical staff or basic equipment such as oxygen or resuscitation devices. I remember sadly a tragic incident in 1967 at Ft. Dix, New Jersey, in which a soldier in my army basic training company had a serious heart attack right after a violently active exercise. The army hospital sent one of these vehicles with only a driver and no oxygen. My classmate died, perhaps before the ambulance arrived, but he had no chance of resuscitation in that vehicle. Had he had one of today's rolling emergency rooms with instant radio communication between trained staff and a cardiologist waiting to receive the patient, he might have lived. Resuscitations are routine events with today's emergency medical teams. Medically trained firefighters are often the first responders to a medical emergency relayed through a 911 telephone call.

Another friend of mine was resuscitated three times in a modern ambulance on the way to the hospital in 2007. He would have died permanently had this happened to him at Ft. Dix in 1967. Because there have been many more resuscitations now than prior to 1970, there are many more near-death experiences to be reported. I heard far more such personally moving accounts thanks to these advances in medical science and practice. And thanks to *Life After Life* and the many books it spawned, many more returnees have had the confidence to talk about their experiences.

## AN ALL-ENCOMPASSING PERSPECTIVE

The more I thought about these accounts, the more I realized I was now looking at all of life through the lens of the insights gained from returnees. I felt the close presence of the Lord. So much understanding in so many arenas opened wide to me. The solid confirmation that *God is,* that *God is loving,* and *really forgiving* brought about a deep peace within me. I never bought another bottle of antacids from that time on. I later threw away an expired, mostly full bottle of them. Several lengthy stays at the Pecos Benedictine Monastery in the mountains of northern New Mexico in the mid-1970s taught me a deeper spirituality. Spiritual direction (the practice of seeking God's word for you with the help of an experienced mentor or group of fellow seekers) became a new vocation in my life, and I have been receiving and teaching it ever since. My long-dead relatives and friends who foresaw and tried to shape an engineering career for me would be astonished to hear me talk about my interests now.

In addition to exploring spirituality, I started to ask hard questions about life. How should we live our lives and make our decisions? As I visited with people who had been mean-spirited and learned about their distressing and, for a few people, hellish near-death experiences, the clarity of Jesus's only commandment was quite clear: live a life of love for God, neighbor, and self. This was the same message of *agapé* love that turned around the fractious parish of which I became pastor at age twenty-nine (*Agapé*—"love"—is the Greek word used by Jesus as reported in the Gospels and by Paul in several of his letters, especially 1 Corinthians 13, his great "Hymn to Love." The word is used to describe the free giving of one's self to the other as a decision *to love*). I was in awe that I had been preaching the very thing the returnees, one after another, said was first and foremost in their meeting with God. Love. This was the case in the subsequent review of their lives. So very many returnees found their lives changed by their experience. They became more compassionate people. Friends and relatives noticed the returnees were far more empathetic, with "rough edges" smoothed. *Agapé* love changes lives. This transition was true for the members of that church in Austin. And it was true in my life as I lived through all these experiences.

As a hospital chaplain, I ministered to dying people and their relatives frequently. Accounts of others' near-death experiences proved immensely helpful and comforting to them. I saw as well the nurses and technicians who, out of their empathy, were also affected by the death of someone with whom they had been working intently. The helpful line Little Fran dropped in Sunday School about when it's "your time" had great impact on the staff who were quietly suffering the loss of one patient after another. I was so pleased to see that the lessons learned were helpful to the long-suffering staff in heading off burnout. Jesus comes and gets you, but he brings you back if it's not your time.

Over the years, as I continued to share stories of near-death experiences with more people, they inevitably started to ask me more and more questions about some of life's thorniest issues. I tried to answer these questions as best I could based on what I gleaned from the accounts of near-death experiences I had heard. Within a few years, however, a new question arose: "What about homosexuals and the next life?"

## THORNY QUESTIONS

There certainly are those who say homosexuals are going to hell for their actions and quote passages from Leviticus, Romans, and 1 Corinthians to support their condemnation. I had not yet visited with any gay or lesbian returnees. So I turned to the Internet and found the Near-Death Experience Research Foundation, led by Jeff Long, M.D., and his wife, Jody. They encouraged a man named Bill to share his near-death experiences with me.

Four of Bill's employees, all of whom were gay, were killed by a drunk driver one night. The driver died too.

Following the accident, Bill had to shoulder all of their workload. As a result, he suffered three fatal heart attacks and went through three near-death experiences. Each time, the four men as well as the drunk driver greeted Bill in heaven. The four gay men obviously hadn't been condemned, and they had forgiven the drunk. That the drunk was there shows me there can be forgiveness after death.

I have since visited with other gay returnees who had a similar beautiful experience upon their deaths as well. In *Crossing Over and Coming Home,* Liz Dale, a clinical psychologist, explores the near-death experiences of twenty-one gay or lesbian returnees.[1] These powerful accounts demonstrate that active homosexuals can have beautiful near-death experiences and aren't condemned to hell for their sexual orientation.

People are also curious about injustice. I know I'm not the only person who gets upset seeing horrifying images on the late news of our inhumanity toward each other: burglars taking valuables from people who haven't much to begin with, murderers, hit-and-run violators, fraudsters, crooked politicians, the perpetrators of various "ethnic cleansings," and so on. "Is there no justice?" I often think after learning of such events.

Then I remember the life review that occurs in typical near-death experiences and realize that an accounting does indeed happen. I take some comfort now, when I watch these reports on the late news, that perfect justice will indeed follow. It is entirely unavoidable.

What about mentally and emotionally ill people who do bad things? I am glad I do not have to judge, but my supposition is that if their illness is the result of maltreatment, the ones responsible for the maltreatment will have to face the results and feel the hurt they caused. That is what numerous returnees have told me on that issue.

I find that accounts of near-death experiences provide a lens through which I can see stunning insights into all aspects of life. It saddens me that there are those who refuse to believe the validity and reality of these reports. They are held hostage by outdated and even harmful attitudes about much in this world and the next. Have I been changed by the near-death experiences I've been privileged to hear? The answer is a resounding "Yes!"

# PART II

# EXPLANATIONS

# 6

# HOW DEATH WORKS

In the years after Alberto shared his near-death experience with me, I have heard or received more than two hundred first-person accounts by people who died and came back. Although many near-death experiences do have a few unique elements, most feature specific themes and universally recognizable patterns. Many closely parallel stories found in the Bible and throughout history. The similarities are unavoidable and fairly consistent. The differences are significant. Some reveal startling new insights into life after death. In every instance, near-death experiences are transcendent and, more often than not, life-changing.

Most experiences proceed along a series of remarkably similar steps as one moves into a continuing life.

My observations include some additional aspects to Moody's model. The most common accounts involve overwhelming feelings of love and peace, highlighted by an encounter with a welcoming being of light, an all-encompassing godlike presence, and being surrounded by beauty and music. As well, there is a joyful reunion with deceased loved ones and pets, a review of one's life and an encounter with angels or spirits, perhaps with a period of instruction. A moment of choice or being told it is not one's time can occur at any point, followed, finally, by a return to the physical body.

Although returnees generally share the same experiences while dead, they tend to approach the moment of death in several distinctly different ways. I cannot comprehend why there are so many; I only observe that, as the accounts have been told to me, there are four main ones. An exceptional fifth way was reported by those who said that Jesus came to get them; these had special ministries to complete that affected many people, including me.

## SPIRITS IN THE ROOM

A quite common beginning step occurs when the dying person recognizes the presence of specific spirits in the room, although no one else present can see them. I have been present several times when the dying perceived individuals in the room no one else could see. They even held conversations with them. The day before my mother died, she turned to me and said, "John, there's someone at the door. Let them in!" There wasn't anyone I could see and told her so. "Yes," she said, "they are there! Let them in, bring them in!" Hospice workers now report this as a common experience with people who are awake in the days prior to their death. My mother certainly could see someone I could not.

Steve Jobs, an entrepreneur and the cofounder of Apple Computer, passed away in 2011. His sister reported that, in his last moments, he looked beyond everyone else in the room, then said, with feeling, "O Wow. O Wow. O Wow." Then he died.[1]

In *One Last Hug Before I Go: The Mystery and Meaning of Deathbed Visions,* Carla Wills-Brandon tells many accounts of people in hospice care with varying experiences of visitors no one else can see, as they move closer to death. She tells of a deathbed vision report from a woman who was with her father when he passed:

> While my father had been confined to his bed, my brother suddenly passed away. His death was most unexpected and very premature. As a family, we elected to withhold this information from my father for as long as we could.
>
> In less than a week's time of my brother's passing, my father said to us, "I used to have three children; now I only have two." There was absolutely no way he could have known my brother had died. . . .
>
> When we asked him why he had said this, he just looked at us as if we were all nuts. Later that week, he finally told us he had seen my brother in a visitation. Along with this, my father made several references to receiving messages from my mother. She had been deceased for fifteen years.[2]

Moody recently published another book on this very aspect of the movement into death, *Glimpses of Eternity*. He relates several accounts, one of which is his own, of people in attendance at a death seeing some portion of the dying person's journey, such as the life review.[3]

## MOVING AWAY FROM THE BODY

A large number of returnees describe leaving their physical body. They often watch the events unfold around them. They can see their former body stretched out in front of them.

Prior to her surgery Julia warned the anesthesiologist about her earlier near-death experience in a dentist's chair following a shot to block pain. The anesthesiologist scoffed at her warning and proceeded anyway. He pointed out that the dentist was neither an M.D. nor a trained anesthesiologist. A dental office, he said, does not have the excellent equipment available in the hospital to prevent such an incident. He assured her it would not happen this time. Nevertheless, the anesthesia again caused her heart to stop. The team pounced on her with electric paddles to restart the cardiac pumping pattern.

"I floated up to the ceiling in the corner of the room," she said, "and watched what they were doing." She saw them administer the paddles and suddenly, "I was back in my body." The heart-stopping painkiller was still in her body, and suddenly, "I was up there again, watching." This happened again and again; her soul floated to the ceiling each time her heart stopped.

Pim van Lommel, a Dutch physician, founder of the International Association for Near-Death Studies in Holland, conducted an experiment in ten hospitals in which a shelf was placed high up in the operating room with cards displaying random letters and numerals. No one could see these cards without climbing a ladder. Patients who had clinically died in the operating room were then interviewed to see what they experienced. Although only 18 percent of cardiac-arrest patients reported a near-death experience, a small percentage of people were able to recall seeing the numbers and letters and reported them *accurately*.[4]

I've also read about people, blind from birth, who shared this experience. They came back to life and gave vivid descriptions of what occurred around their bodies. This included colors and other visual details they could not have known in their physical body. Their accounts tell me the spiritual body, as opposed to the earthly body, remains intact in this new realm, free of all physical handicaps. Many of these accounts are included in the well-written *Mindsight: Near-Death and Out-of-Body Experiences in the Blind,* by Kenneth Ring and Sharon Cooper.[5]

It needs to be said at this point that many returnees did not immediately understand they were dead. The fact of their death came to them as an astounding realization. Perhaps this explains people's spirits that do not go on to heaven; some may not realize they are dead and stay in the vicinity of their death. They may well appear as "ghosts," such as the one who shows all the signs of having been a victim of the 1900 hurricane in Galveston, Texas. This specter appeared at the previous William Temple Foundation facility near the University of Texas Medical School. Many perfectly reasonable, educated people, staff members at the facility, for instance, told me they had seen this woman in Victorian dress, distraught, saying repeatedly, "They are coming for me," as if she still expected to be rescued. Obviously rescuers didn't come. Accounts of the storm tell about buildings falling over on people, obscuring the bodies. Thus she may well have not seen her body to realize she had been killed.

In 1943, George Ritchie was a twenty-year-old enlisted man suffering from pneumonia in an army hospital. He had an extensive near-death experience and related that it was quite some "time" before he realized he had died. He told of repeatedly trying to talk to hospital orderlies who wouldn't respond to him, and he wondered who it was who was in his bed. Ritchie's story inspired his friend Raymond Moody to research the phenomenon and write his book *Life After Life.* Ritchie subsequently wrote his own book, *Return From Tomorrow,* which was published in 1978.[6]

Pam Reynolds, a brain-tumor patient I read about on the IANDS website, underwent a rare surgical procedure called Operation Standstill. Doctors drained the blood from her system and lowered her body temperature to 60 degrees. In the process, her brain, heart, and organ functions all ceased. While anesthetized, she came to while the surgeon was cutting into her skull. The sound of the electronic saw woke her. She started to observe the procedure from over the surgeon's shoulder. She could also overhear what the nurses said to the doctor. When she regained consciousness, she accurately described the events in full detail.

Kimberly Clark Sharp, a Seattle social worker, told IANDS about her experience in 1995. A woman named Marie was brought to the hospital following a cardiac arrest. Sharp visited her the next day. Marie told her she left her body and floated above the hospital. When Kimberly doubted her story, Marie described a worn dark blue tennis shoe on the ledge outside of a window on the other side of the hospital. Kimberly decided to humor her. When she looked for the shoe, she found it—exactly the way Marie had described it.

## FLOATING THROUGH A TUNNEL AND SEEING A LIGHT

The feeling of floating through a tunnel is the most common movement associated with near-death experiences. Alberto described moving through a tunnel with a buzzing sound before meeting a "dude made of light." Some medical professionals try to explain this away as a result of anoxia, a lack of oxygen. They insist that the brain in this condition is playing tricks on the mind, causing hallucinations. Approximately 40 percent of the accounts told to me report *only* this element of the experience before the people are back in the body. Although anoxic illusions might rationalize away some brief near-death experiences, they do not explain the details of the other 60 percent of the accounts I heard, including the other varied means of exiting the body or the stages that follow. I also find that, among the medical professionals with whom I've spoken, those who are regularly involved with resuscitations generally believe these accounts. Medical personnel who are not involved with resuscitations tend to doubt, disbelieve, or discount these stories out of hand. All exceptions are granted, but these are the patterns.

Since many medical personnel discount the "tunnel and light" variation to be the result of anoxia, I discount these out of deference to them. Beyond this stage, near-death events cannot be so easily dismissed. Even if I discard and ignore these relatively simple accounts, there are over 120 left for me to consider.

## STANDING UP AND WALKING AROUND

I met Ian while working on a near-death lecture on a computer. He was helping me figure out a problem with the program. On my computer screen, he saw what I was writing about. He said, "I think I had one of those experiences." With my encouragement, he continued:

> I was riding with a friend and he was driving too fast, really, when a gravel truck in front of us had stopped and we slammed into it. Our subcompact car was destroyed, and my lower legs were badly broken as the engine came into them. The radio in the dashboard went through the rear window, which tells you something about how bad the wreck was.
>
> I was blinded by this terrific light and covered my eyes. I was out walking around the car with my hands over my eyes. These people were talking to me, but I don't remember what they said. Then I woke up in the ambulance.

He was physically walking around with two badly smashed legs? I pointed out to him that that would have been impossible in his physical body, but not in his spiritual body.

A dying friend, George, once told me about the time his grandfather and father appeared at the end of the bed with an unknown third person,

> a being that was an incredibly bright light, like that of an arc welder, standing at the foot of the bed with my father and grandfather. I stood up on the bed to greet

> them. My father and grandfather smiled and told me it wasn't my time yet.

Remarkably, George told me he stood up on the bed to greet them, even though he was missing one leg and had many tubes and wires going in and out of his body. He was even restrained. It could never have happened in the physical life. The restraints alone would have held him down. His missing leg would not have allowed him to stand. None of these features were true of the now complete "spiritual body" in which he greeted his loved ones. George lived another few months and died at home.

## JESUS CAME AND GOT ME

My parishioner Ella said, "Jesus came through the ceiling, held his hands down to me, and I lifted my hands to him. He lifted me up through the ceiling."

Lou, the aunt of a friend, saw Jesus at the end of her bed in the intensive-care unit. "Don't be afraid," he said. "You have not lived as you should have lived. I want you to come to me and bring your husband, and bring your children."

Little Fran, at age three and a half, pointed to a specific hospital and said matter-of-factly, "Oh, look, Mommy, that's where Jesus brought me back to you." The event had happened in her eighth *week* of life. "You know, Mommy, Jesus came and got me, but he brought me back to you there." She later said in Sunday School at age four and again at five, "When you die, Jesus comes and gets you, but if it's not your time, he brings you back." I have repeatedly used Fran's account pastorally to help people facing death—either their own or a loved one's—understand there is "a time" for each of us. Medical staff also appreciate this insight when a patient has died they were trying to keep alive. It makes the point that you can have the best staff, pharmaceuticals, facility, equipment, funding, and dedication, but when it is someone's "time," there is no standing in the way of his or her death. I tell them to "do the best you can," but do not feel as if the death was a defeat.

This element of Jesus coming to get the dying person's soul is not frequent in my experience. But it is one of the five different means by which the soul departs, or gets ready to depart, the body. There must be something special about those whom Jesus comes specifically to get and escort to heaven. Fran was a baby whose testimony became a very significant part of my pastoral ministry. Ella had a special role to play in the life of our church during her one more week of life here. Lou and her husband started a new church in which the powers of God are not doubted, and they have a powerful healing ministry.

After listening to all of these accounts of death, I now know that there is very little to fear about dying. Most of the returnees I have met with or counseled tell me they no longer even fear death, because they know what awaits them on the other side. Death, then, loses its power over them.

# 7

# HOW HEAVEN WORKS

Heaven, returnees tell us, is beautiful. Mary C. Neal, a board-certified orthopedic surgeon who drowned while kayaking in Chile, described her arrival in heaven as "joyously celebrated"; she said, "A feeling of absolute love was palpable as [spirits] and I hugged, danced, and greeted each other." The intensity of these feelings, she writes in her wonderful book *To Heaven and Back*, exceed both her power of description and anything she ever experienced on earth.[1]

Similarly, Colton Burpo told his father, Todd, as Todd reports in *Heaven Is for Real*, that heaven is where you reunite with your family, a special place peopled by Jesus and angels, where "nobody is old and nobody wears glasses."[2] Mary's and Colton's descriptions of heaven are in line with the accounts I've heard firsthand from returnees.

Dirk Willner, a Lutheran pastor in Australia, told me: "I emerged out of darkness in front of this huge mansion. Golden, honey-colored light streamed out of the windows and surrounded me, pushing back the darkness. The golden light saturated my every cell, my very being. It also had a presence to it, but different from the darkness." Like Mary, Dirk said the joy he felt at that moment was "more real and intense" than any emotion he had ever had in his best moments on earth. In an e-mail, he recounted his first few moments in heaven:

> At first my eyes were overpowered by the brilliance inside, but after a brief moment I was able to see this large hall filled with people, all dressed in white. The place sparkled, there was a golden staircase at the rear of this hall leading to other sections, and it had a very festive mood. Everything had an extra dimension to things. Everything looked more real. I remember taking note of how people looked—and the only explanation that I have is that I was able to see round. When we see people normally, we only get to see

what they want to reveal. This was like seeing people for who they are—as God sees them: all at once. Also the white gowns were part of people; it wasn't like they had put clothing on as a separate fabric, but that it was an extension of who they were, like the robe of salvation, or the gown of righteousness, from scripture. They all looked young, but were not young in age, just freed from the decay and curse of death; fully alive.

Julia, the woman who went through two near-death experiences following her exposure to anesthesia, told me that in both experiences her grandfather greeted her. A child of alcoholic parents, Julia didn't have much of a relationship with her immediate family. Some relatives even tried to scare her into joining their fundamentalist church by threatening that Jesus would "get her" if she didn't. Her grandfather was the only peaceful, positive family she remembered. Religion for Julia was fear-based. Eventually, she found some peace in Buddhism and remains a Buddhist today. When Julia died, her grandfather greeted her both times, representing the most godlike person in her life. He then introduced her to many of her dead relatives she had never known.

When she recovered from her first near-death event at age eighteen, she told me, she recounted her experience for her mother. Fascinated, her mother took out the family's photo album to show Julia a few pictures. Julia was able to name everyone she saw, even though most had passed away well before she was born. As if this weren't amazing enough, she told her mother, "Someone is missing. His name is James." Her mother brought down a photograph of her great-grandfather James. "That's not him," Julia insisted. "James is a young man." Her mother then retrieved a picture of a much younger James, whom Julia accurately identified.

Colton Burpo's father relates a conversation with four-year-old Colton about meeting his great-grandfather, who had died long before the boy was born:

> Colton spoke up. "Dad, you had a grandpa named Pop, didn't you?"
>
> "Yep, I sure did," I said.
>
> "Was he your mommy's daddy or your daddy's daddy?"
>
> "Pop was my mom's dad. He passed away when I was not much older than you."
>
> Colton smiled. "He's really nice."

I almost drove off the road into the corn. It's a crazy moment when your son uses the present tense to refer to someone who died a quarter of a century before he was even born. But I tried to stay cool.

"So you saw Pop?" I said.

"Yeah, I got to stay with him in heaven. You were really close to him, huh, Dad?"

"Yes, I was," was all I could manage. My head spun. Colton had just introduced a whole new topic: people you've lost, and meeting them in heaven. . . .

"When I was a little boy," I said, "I had a lot of fun with Pop. . . . I spent a lot of time with Pop at their place out in the country," I said to Colton. "I rode on the combine and the tractor with him. . . ."

Colton nodded again: "Yeah, I know! Pop told me."[3]

Stories such as these—and the ones that follow below—leave little doubt about the love, warmth, and greatness of heaven—Paradise—and the glorious moments and emotions it offers us. When we die, a series of specific surprises or stages awaits us, but not everyone goes through all of them. A soul can be told, "It's not your time" at any point along the journey, and it returns instantly.

## A BEING OF LIGHT

Many returnees told me they were immediately in the presence of "a being made of light, not flesh and bone," just as Alberto and George experienced. The light emanating from this being, according to the returnees, was very intense. My friend George described it as "the brightness of an arc welder's spark all over the body." To my surprise, however, George told me it didn't hurt his eyes. Many identified the being as Jesus. Some merely described what they saw, while others said it was a "spiritual being." Hua, an Asian American Buddhist, said she was not aware of any name or title, but she knew she "was in the presence of God."

I visited an Orthodox rabbi and asked if he'd spoken with anyone who had a near-death experience. "My wife," he said. "She went through a tunnel and saw a light, but was back immediately." That was the extent of the experience for her. Coming back can happen at any point along the journey.

Ian told me after the wreck he shielded his eyes from a blinding light, got out of the car, and walked around through a group of people, but didn't pay attention to what they said.

## A REUNION WITH LOVED ONES

After meeting the being of light, most returnees say they reunited with deceased loved ones and friends who greeted them joyously and lovingly, just as Colton and Julia said happened when they were in heaven. Julia told me she saw her beloved dead cats. In addition to meeting his grandfather, Colton also met his "other sister," the child his mother and father lost to a miscarriage before her birth. They had never told Colton about her. Alberto told me at length about seeing in heaven his grandfather and old friends from his San Antonio neighborhood.

A startling and convincing aspect of this portion of the experience is that some ran into a loved one they didn't know was dead. When resuscitated, they reported seeing a specific person who others didn't know had died. Or in some cases the persons present had not told the dying one of the other's demise. Iris, a retired British registered nurse, told me that in her training days, an empathetic doctor administered a fatal dose of morphine to a badly suffering patient. The patient dropped into a deep sleep, and her breathing slowed. Iris said:

I thought she had died, but later she began breathing more normally. When she awoke, she began talking, telling me she thought she had died and gone to heaven. "But it couldn't have been heaven, because I saw my daughter there, and she is alive." However, she was unaware that her daughter *had* died that night in a car accident. The doctor decided to tell her what had happened to her daughter. "Then I really did die, and was in heaven, Doctor?" she asked. He agreed, and she dropped into a contented sleep, one from which she never awoke in this world.

## A LIFE REVIEW

Returnees also describe an extensive review of their life, from birth until death, as if they're watching a live reenactment of their time on earth. During the review they felt the emotions of others when they watched their interactions. They felt the hurt of a cruel action they caused as well as the happiness or comfort they brought to another person by an act of compassion.

After drowning at age eight, Harold told me that he saw himself earlier that year scratching the paint on a new car with his house key. The scratch was lengthy, along the car's side, deep into the paint. Then, still in the review of his life, he saw the owner of the car, sorely distressed that his first new car had been so badly scratched. Harold felt deeply the anguish of the car's owner. Additionally, he felt the sadness of the man's wife when she saw that noticeable scratch on their first new car. Harold was filled with remorse for what he had done, but he also felt forgiven.

Many people report that things they had been told not to do on earth were not even issues during the review and certainly did not require forgiveness. This includes dancing, drinking alcohol (moderately, presumably), swearing, masturbation, homosexual sex, using birth control, skipping church, not being baptized, not being an active member of a church, and even not being a Christian. I have spoken with Buddhists and Jeff, an unbaptized returnee who is now a Christian, all of whom had positive experiences. All these people told me the review of their lives was done in love and warmth and with forgiveness.

Love and forgiveness. These are the key elements we hear repeatedly of the life review in heaven. These are the important facts to know about God. From what the returnees tell us, loving and forgiving are how we are to live as well. Criticism in the review of one's life comes as a consequence of acts that do not reflect those values or that behavior. Recall Jesus's prayer: "And forgive us our sins, for we ourselves forgive everyone indebted to us" (Luke 11:4). Recall Jesus's only commandment: "Love one another as I have loved you" (John 15:12). Recall Jesus telling the lawyer that the first and greatest commandment is, "Love the Lord your God with all your heart, and with all your soul, and with all your mind," and the second is, "Love your neighbor as yourself" (Matthew 22:37, 39).

When I am explaining Christianity to someone, I make the point from both the Bible and near-death experiences that these are the main elements of Christianity. Christianity is a religion of love, not law, and certainly not of fear. This statement of mine is based on scripture, but corroborated by various near-death experiences and borne out in life experiences.

## A PERIOD OF INSTRUCTION

Although uncommon, a limited number of returnees told me about meeting with angels or even Jesus for an intense period of instruction, during which time great wisdom and truth were imparted to them. In his book *My Descent into Death,* Howard Storm describes this event movingly:

> In my conversation with Jesus and the angels, they told me about God. I asked them what God is like and they told me this: God knows everything that will happen and, more important, God knows everything that could happen. From one moment to the next, God is aware of every possible variable of every event and each outcome. God doesn't control or dictate the outcome of every event, which would be a violation of God's creation.[4]

Often returnees can't recall what they heard. Recall that Paul said, "I know that this man . . . was caught up to paradise and heard inexpressible things, things that no one is permitted to tell" (2 Corinthians 12:3–4, NIV). The returnees with whom I spoke who had gone through a period of instruction knew that it had happened, but simply could not remember what they were told.

But Dirk Willner told me angels visited him a full week after his near-death experience:

> I was sitting having a chat with God about my bewilderment about the near-death experience and what its purpose might be. Then suddenly there were five angels standing around my bed. They were larger than a human figure and full of sparkles. The one on my right side said to me, "What instructions have you got for us?"
>
> I responded, "Instruction? If you want instructions, you need to see God about them; I don't have any instructions for you."
>
> He then asked me to put my hand to his. He reached out his hand, and I remember thinking, "Well, I'll see where this will go." Once I had my hand in his, I then spoke in a strange heavenly language to him. God was speaking into my mind not to be worried about this, because it's scriptural and God is speaking his instruction through me to these angels. I then placed my hand in each of the other angels' hands and spoke

a different language with each one of them. I can still speak all five languages even after these six months have passed.

They then disappeared, and I noticed one other angel who wasn't there before sitting on my bed. I asked him what I could do for him, and his reply was, "Nothing. I'm just here for you!" We smiled at each other and that was that.

## A MOMENT OF DECISION

Some returnees arrived at a "fence" or "barrier," where they were told they had a choice to either return or stay. Others were told it was "not their time." This happened to Alberto. While on the other side, he got to the fence, and "the dude in white" told him he had to return. This moment of forced departure can happen at any point along the near-death continuum, from exiting the body up through the period of instruction.

Many wanted to stay in this new, beautiful place, but were refused and woke up in their bodies. Some were really angry at being resuscitated. Others, like Kay, who survived a drowning at the age of three, were offered a choice between staying or returning to earth. She decided to go back because loved ones needed her:

> I had the real feeling that I was given a choice. I made the choice to come back, maybe because of the pain I knew my death would cause my mother. There was nothing right or wrong about this, just that I had a choice.

During her second near-death experience under anesthetics, Julia, the American Buddhist we met earlier, was pronounced dead forty-five minutes after the medical staff repeatedly tried to shock her back to life. The postmortem procedures began. The surgeon and anesthesiologist drafted her death certificate and completed the other paperwork detailing the procedures they had accomplished. Nurses prepared the body for the morgue. A team removed her body from the operating room. Again, her grandfather and other deceased relatives greeted Julia, all of whom she had met in her near-death experience ten years earlier. Just as they did before, they told her it was not yet her time. She had to go back.

As her spirit reentered her body, she saw a clipboard on her physical body's chest—fastened to it was her death certificate! She began speaking. At this, the morgue workers ran in fright. Meanwhile, the anesthesiologist was coming down to the morgue, remorseful about this patient who had warned him of her sensitivity to anesthesia. He was astonished to discover she was alive. Later Julia asked for the death certificate, but of course it had been destroyed by then. However, other records of her death still exist.

During his time in heaven, Dirk encountered an unknown man who welcomed him with enthusiasm and delight. Dirk said:

> He had a crystal goblet in his hand, with a golden ring around it, filled with red wine to overflowing. He offered it to me and said that it was my cup. Before I reached out to take hold of it, however, another man approached him and whispered something into his ear. The man with the goblet then turned back to me and said, "Oh, it looks like you'll just be a moment, so I'll put this cup of wine to the side here, and it will be waiting for you when you return."

A few minutes later, Dirk returned to his body.

Several others asked if they could return. These

were allowed to resume life on earth because of some unfulfilled duty such as raising their children or tending to an ill spouse. This does not answer the question of why others who died, despite having children, did not return.

Some people with whom I've spoken were really angry with the medical staff for resuscitating them. They were brought back from the most loving, peaceful experience they had ever known to a body wracked with pain and all the accompanying difficulties of life. Robert, a former fundamentalist preacher, remains angry that he was brought back to life. He calls this earthly life "hell" by comparison. Now he doesn't have the credentials or education to work in a church that would understand and accept his change of heart.

Because most of us haven't experienced heaven, we do not fully understand the immense joy and love with which our returnee friends were met there. They experience a feeling of deep peace and of being "home." Often they feel residual anger about their forced return, which is often compounded by any physical pain from their fatal injuries. Returnees also sometimes face implicit or explicit rejection from family and friends who don't believe their accounts.

# 8

# HELLISH EXPERIENCES

But what about hell? Do any returnees report nightmarish experiences that some might call "hell"? The answer is yes. Twelve people have related to me near-death experiences ranging from distressing to utterly hellish. They did not have a beautiful, peaceful experience at all. Nine of them were mean-spirited, cruel people. Following their encounters, seven of those turned their lives around. One died a few days later and, to the best of my knowledge, had no chance to alter the course of his life. I never saw or heard from the other person again.

## NINE REPORTS

Diana was the first person to tell me about her distressing near-death experience. Responsible for running off five priests in our parish before I arrived in 1968, Diana was an entirely different person when I met her. I only knew the "new Diana," though horror stories about the "old Diana" were well known.

Her notorious husband died during my immediate predecessor's tenure. Shortly thereafter, she suffered a major heart attack. One night in the hospital she had another cardiac event during which she encountered the long-dead founder of our parish. She later told me:

> Reverend Brewster appeared in my room in all his vestments and asked me sternly if I was ready to see God. "No-o-o!" I replied, in remorse for all I had done. He told me I had another chance to make it good.

Diana subsequently became a warm, loving person, genuinely caring for others, and welcomed visitors warmly to the church as a one-person greeting committee. Her son, however, continued to abuse alcohol. Realizing the change in his mother and their new relationship, he joined Alcoholics Anonymous and turned his life around. By the time I arrived five years later, he was a solid contributing member of the parish and became a lifelong friend; his mother Diana remained a dear, sweet woman.

A fellow officer in the Texas Army National Guard relayed his uncle's troubling account. In hushed tones, the uncle related, "I was going down a black tunnel, naked, screaming, with lots of other naked, screaming people, and all of us were clawing at the walls of the black tunnel."

"Uncle," the officer replied in great awe, "you were going to hell. You need to accept Jesus Christ as Savior and ask for his help." The uncle died three days later, and we do not know the state of his soul before or after his death.

A soldier recently returned from combat in Vietnam told me the third account. He was one of many of our soldiers who had become entranced with their firepower and, as he put it, were just "popping gooks." There was a mortar attack, and he was hit badly. He said:

> I found myself struggling along in a ditch full of the blood, guts, and brains of people I'd shot, with them

> up on the top of the ditch, missing limbs, sides of their heads, faces, and so on, screaming and pointing at me.

Then the medics plugged the gaping wound and gave him CPR and a transfusion, and he woke up in his body, terrified. He changed and became deeply concerned for others.

In his book *My Descent into Death*, Howard Storm, an atheist and professor of art at a Kentucky college, told of his full-blown near-death experience. A vicious person on earth, he was in utter torment until he cried out, "Jesus, help me!" At that point Jesus scattered the demons and he met with angels in heaven. The conversation changed his life. His is an outstanding book on the subject of distressing experiences.

The fifth was a very difficult person whose first marriage failed because of his inability to relate. Following a distressing near-death experience of his own, he subsequently married a woman who, as well, had a near-death experience. Now he is an M.D., largely treating patients who can't afford to pay for medical treatment. He said:

> Following the experience there were enormous transformations in my life. I had a "spiritual experience,"

though I was not sure what that meant. Before the experience I was relatively unpleasant, proud, and aloof, among other negative attributes. After I began thinking about my experience, I changed quite substantially, and began a rather passionate search to understand the spiritual.

A medical doctor with an uncontrollable temper was number six. He had a heart attack during which he met a spiritual being who sternly warned him to control his anger. He has since become a warm, friendly person very supportive of near-death studies.

The seventh suffered a heart attack. In his hospital room across the street from the church, the man asked for an Episcopal priest. Our church was called, the secretary passed the request to me, and I went to see him in the coronary-care unit. He told me in great anxiety of his distressing experience, but steadfastly refused to go into detail. "What did this mean?" he asked, on the verge of sobbing.

I told him that the six others I'd spoken to at that point who had a similar experience were truly mean people. He burst into tears, admitting that he knew he was fiercely callous. He swore to change his life.

We prayed together for his future, but I never saw him again. My guess is that he was too ashamed to share his life's review or perhaps his punishment. I pray that in whatever time he had left he was able to take the measures necessary to alter the course of his life.

It is heavy stuff, visiting with people who've been to hell and have returned. It gets worse. The eighth story was from a prisoner who told me of the incredibly terrible childhood he had—abusive treatment and drug addiction in a thoroughly dysfunctional family. Since this abusive pattern was "normal" for him, it was how he then treated others. His life fell apart as the drug abuse, drug pushing, and life of crime came together in capture, trial, and a prison sentence. It culminated in his committing suicide hara-kiri style, slicing himself open with a knife from below the navel up to the rib cage.

Immediately he found himself in utter torment. He was tied up, bitten, and torn apart by a ferocious demon who looked very much like a *Tyrannosaurus rex*. At one point the demon itself showed fear and awe, cringing as a very powerful spirit figure appeared. This figure bellowed, "Because you have done this, you will be cut off from me forever! *Forever!*" In the midst of this episode the prisoner cried out, "Lord, help me!" and apologized profusely for his behavior.

In the next instant he was in a hospital bed, with a pretty young nurse standing over him, assuring him he was okay. "We lost you for a while, but you're going to be all right now."

Later in the day another, older nurse came to check on him and told him, "You're going to be all right; we lost you for a while, but you're going to live. We've just never seen anyone live whose liver has been so lacerated."

He later inquired about the pretty young nurse, and the staff was puzzled. There was no such person. His assumption now is that she must have been an angel. So when the angel said, "We lost you for a while," she didn't just mean the cessation of his vital signs. She meant that he had been lost from God's ways and given over to hellish ways.

After his release from prison, we discussed the viciously angry spiritual being who told the man he was "cut off" from him "forever." He thought this was God. I told him I did not think so at all—I thought this was Satan. The devil, consummate liar that he is, can masquerade as an angel of light, but his malevolence comes through. God is love and would not be so maliciously condemnatory. Remember, when the prisoner called out to the Lord for relief, it came.

The ninth person was a gracious, now deeply religious woman who told me about her distressing near-death experience. Others told me she was a scurrilous person prior to her experience. When suffering from the effects of pneumonia, she exited her body and was in a very black tunnel. There was no light at the end as usually reported, only a frightening blackness. She kept calling to the Lord for light. Light came, as she was shown a pit with flames leaping out. A voice asked if she wanted to go down there or to go back. "I know that's hell. I don't want to go there! I learned that in Sunday School. I don't want to go there. I want to go back."

The experience turned her life around. No longer is she a bitter, angry, continually complaining, unforgiving woman. She is now an exuberant Spirit-filled person, using her energy to heal others. She was shown that pit with flames and was told she could either go into the pit or return to life and change. She chose to go back.

These are nine of the twelve people with whom I've spoken who had distressing or hellish near-death experiences. Some of them were active, respected members of churches, but despite their church involvement, they had distressing experiences. I've known plenty of such controlling, mean-spirited people in churches over the years, heard of plenty more, and wondered about their experiences at death. We have to be empathetic toward them, however; there is always hope for their conversion. After all, we do not want to act as mean-spiritedly as they do. A distressing near-death experience might be the best therapy or recovery program someone can have.

## TWO TYPES

There are two types of distressing experiences. The simple one features a serious warning that the deceased has not lived in accordance with Jesus's insistence on love. Such people typically have a negative reputation and have a brief corrective event with a rapid return to the body. After such an event, they change their behavior in a manner that has a great impact on the people around them.

Was what they experienced a dream or a hallucination? I've not seen lives changed as dramatically from a mere dream. And a life filled with hallucinations is going to have its own patterns that have an even more negative impact on friends and loved ones. No, the lives of these returnees are far more normal after the experience. Their offensive behavior is a thing of the past, and their ability to empathize, typically missing before the experience, appears in abundance afterward.

The second type is the more dramatic and utterly negative experience of torment and punishment from wild demons that captures the imagination with visions of hell and eternal punishment. The changes in behavior and belief in persons who experience this are quite dramatic.

# 9

# THE RETURN

After a wonderful experience in heaven, the return to the physical world with all its attendant problems—bills, illness, dysfunctional relationships—is often an enormous letdown. Returnees often report feeling overwhelmed by both joy and fear. They know that what they went through was real, but they often remain reluctant to share this experience with others. In my experience, the return is often the most difficult part of the entire near-death phenomenon, though the returnees I spoke with all describe coming back with a refreshed outlook on life and in possession of newfound abilities.

## A RETURN TO THE BODY

After their near-death experience, many returnees move quickly back into their bodies. A few returnees have told me Jesus or an angel gently led them back to their physical form. At this point, the returnees became very aware of any pain or extreme temperature.

Anita Moorjani is a Hindu from India. She tells of her death from a long debilitating bout with cancer. In her near-death experience, she was told it was not her time and she had to go back. She argued that her body was thoroughly depleted and could not live long. "You will be healed," she was told. She reluctantly returned. Anita indeed recovered with great difficulty and now travels the world relating her experience and her mystical conclusions about life.[1]

Most people with whom I've spoken were resuscitated, although some spontaneously came back to life, like Ella and Julia. Alberto also spontaneously came back to life. He awoke in his body with his buddies slapping him. In his book *Ninety Minutes in Heaven,* Don Piper tells of his spontaneous return to life after the emergency techs had declared him dead.[2] A friend went back to pray for him and saw signs of life. He tried to summon the medical team, who disbelieved him and scoffed. Finally, to placate the friend, they went back to the car and realized Piper was alive.

## AN ALTERED VIEW OF LIFE, DEATH, AND GOD

Returnees often come back with an altered view of life. They no longer fear death and, more often than not, believe thoroughly, with no doubts, in the existence of God. For the most part, returnees feel a strong sense of purpose in life, with heightened self-esteem. Their profound, cherished experience almost always alters returnees' lives so thoroughly that their whole approach to life changes radically. They become more altruistic and empathetic. Roger Cilley, late suffragan bishop of the diocese of Texas, was in a horrific automobile accident in 1953 when he was still teaching drama at the University of Texas. He died on the operating table, but was eventually resuscitated. Afterward, he told me he no longer feared death. The experience led him to enter the seminary in 1954.

Tess was a college student when her boyfriend raped

her. During the attack, he choked her unconscious. She told me:

> I was sound asleep and woke up to find he was raping me and had his hands around my neck, strangling me. I remember being momentarily shocked, because it made no sense, and there was no precipitating fight, and also because his face was so contorted. His features actually looked demonic, and I had never seen anything like that before. His eyes were even yellowish, instead of brown. I started fighting him, but he was a big guy and I couldn't budge his hands. It didn't take long before I quit fighting and started to lose consciousness. I couldn't believe that my life was going to end so abruptly and at such a young age. I thought, "Wow, it's all over. I'm going to die now," and suddenly and seamlessly I was over my body up near the ceiling.
>
> I looked down at the young woman on the bed being raped and killed and felt sorry for her, but had no emotional connection to her. It was like my body belonged to someone else. I was surprised at how comfortable I was, and how easy it was to die. It all happened within a couple of minutes. I said to myself, "Huh, I thought that one was supposed to last longer,"

> and headed up in a light cloud. It felt so perfect. I felt like I was going home, and I felt comfortable and joyous with no doubts at all. It was like every cell of my body was happy and light and felt right, and I have never felt so accepted. I started rising rapidly, which was weird because I don't remember seeing any roofs, but I must have been far over my house. I didn't care about my family, friends, beloved pets, or my murderer; I just wanted to float in my light of happiness and go home.
>
> Suddenly, I hit an invisible wall, and I felt like I was slammed back into my body.

After her near-death experience, Tess, who grew up around the Roman Catholic Church, said her faith was solidified:

> I was raised by a sneering atheist father, agnostic mother, and strict Catholic grandmother. I went to church and drove my grandmother and the nuns crazy with questions about God, Jesus, and religion. At age twelve, I encountered something black that flew through the closed window and scared me, and I prayed to Mother Mary to save me. The room filled

> with light, and the black thing vanished. I knew without a doubt that there was a God, who was good, and there was evil. It was established in my mind as irrefutable truth. I never had to wonder if there was a God, or wonder if God would protect me if I needed.
>
> I had a pretty open, but strong religious belief, albeit unconventional, before the near-death experience. It just made it unshakable, unquestionable, and so much a part of my life.

Like Bishop Roger Cilley, Tess no longer fears death. This, she says, is the biggest change:

> I have women friends who go around scared all the time. I just don't. I fear pain and injury because I have been badly hurt and had many surgeries, but I really am not afraid of much. I wouldn't hesitate for a nanosecond to lay down my life for another. I often discover that I am already in motion toward a threat before my brain has a chance to send a danger signal. Having fear cripples you in so many areas of your life.
>
> I certainly am not afraid of dying. I will welcome it. God will take care of me, no matter what. I worry less now and assume it will all work out.

## NEWFOUND ABILITIES

A few people, returning from death, report the disturbing ability to read the minds of those around them. This fact often causes great personal distress, and they try to squelch this new gift. Others report being able to see events in the future, which often come true. A few report a facility to heal through prayer and touch. This, of course, is taught in Christian theology and the New Testament. In John 14:12 Jesus says, "Very truly, I tell you, the one who believes in me will also do the works that I do and, in fact, will do greater works than these, because I am going to the Father." According to Luke, Jesus sent out seventy-two disciples to pray and heal. They "returned with joy, saying, 'Lord, in your name even the demons submit to us!'" (10:17).

A few returnees tell of visits from angels and holding discussions with them, a fact most people have a hard time believing. After his near-death experience, Dirk Willner told me he regularly feels the presence of angels around him. He believes they continue to help him in his ministry.

Tess claims to now have a heightened sense of catastrophe:

Mostly I hear a voice telling me about someone, or I feel energy coming from someone. Sometimes the voice is in my head, but separate from my usual voice. The voice is sometimes male, has been disembodied, in the room with me, and sounds like an invisible person.

When I tried to tell my mother she needed to go to the hospital because she was going to die, I heard an invisible young man next to me say, "You will never speak to her again." Then my mother had company arrive and abruptly hung up the phone. She died that night. I have figured out that I can't change a thing like death.

I told a cop friend of mine that I smelled death around him. He died of a sudden heart attack a month later. I hope he said what he needed to to his family because of it.

## AN UNCOMMON SOURCE OF ENERGY

Over Labor Day weekend 2011, I went to the International Association of Near-Death Studies' thirtieth annual conference in Durham, North Carolina. During the first plenary session, I noticed an odd thing: my iPhone would not bring up my e-mail. Strangely, it had worked earlier in the morning while I was still in my hotel room. The signal strength was ample. About an hour later, I tried again and noticed something even stranger: the iPhone's battery was rapidly losing its power. It was not going to last even until lunch. Its battery has always lasted all day. I had not been using it while listening to the lectures. Thinking I had too many programs working simultaneously, I turned off all others, but to no avail. Finally, at the next break, I turned it off altogether. I charged its battery over the lunch hour and was again able to get my e-mail while in my hotel room.

Later that afternoon, Mitchell Liester, M.D., in an afternoon announcement, explained that returnees often have a puzzling predicament: they can no longer wear an ordinary wristwatch without ruining it. One woman, shocked at the revelation, said with some dismay, "I've gone through *five*!" Whether the returnees develop a strong magnetic field or excess electricity is not clear. Liester is currently conducting an extensive study with returnees and others around them. I later learned there were ninety-nine returnees in the conference room when I was having the strange difficulties with my iPhone. When I left the vicinity of large numbers of returnees, the difficulties cleared up. I anxiously await Liester's findings.

## A RELUCTANCE TO SHARE THEIR EXPERIENCES

Some people talked readily about their near-death experience until they realized people thought they were hallucinating or "out of their mind." For others, the experience was just too intimate to share, and they feared being ridiculed, laughed at, or thought deluded, insane, you name it. Our quick-to-react society can be insensitive to those who have had an intangible experience others do not share and are not inclined to believe. Too many returnees have told me they keep this part of their life hidden, lest they be considered a kook or a liar. It is unfortunate that those like Lou don't feel free to reveal everything they have learned. If they could, I believe, they would bring others to a deeper knowledge of God and his plan for our lives.

Lou's near-death experience did not follow the usual pattern. As we heard earlier, she says Jesus simply appeared at the end of her bed in the intensive-care unit. "Don't be afraid," he told her lovingly. "You have not lived as you should have lived. I want you to come to me and bring your husband, and bring your children."

She knew it was Jesus. He didn't have to tell her who he was; he simply, very lovingly, in a noncondemnatory way, made that simple statement. Because of her poor health, however, she hesitated to tell her husband, an alcoholic, about her near-death experience. Their marriage was tenuous at best, and Lou didn't want to do anything to bring it crashing down. She didn't know what to do, though the event had a dramatic impact on her life.

She tried to tell her minister, but he would have none of it. She left that church and found another, one that accepted her and her story. A year later, she and her husband were in a discussion group in which the participants were asked to share a spiritual experience they had had in the past. At this point, she felt she could talk about it. Her husband became quite animated and said, "I *knew* it! I *knew* something had happened to you!"

She and her husband, now fully recovered with the help of Alcoholics Anonymous, have since helped start several churches. They are currently living very happily in their retirement, true disciples of Christ. "I did not have a personal relationship with the Lord before," she said. "Now I do."

Lonnie, a handsome fifteen-year-old boy from a suburb of Houston, got caught in a thunderstorm on a golf course. A lightning bolt struck him in the upper chest. A man who lived at the edge of the golf course ran to him and successfully administered CPR. The man was not supposed to have been at his house that Tuesday afternoon. The emergency medical team flew Lonnie to a leading trauma care center in Houston, where he lingered near death for days. The clergy from our church across the street from the hospital were recommended to Lonnie and his family and began visiting them in the hospital. Grateful for the almost daily pastoral care, the family began to attend our church services on occasion, since they were now spending a great deal of time in the Texas Medical Center.

Lonnie recovered sufficiently to come to church, where he became a celebrity. Though he was unable to speak, he remained a very happy young man, always smiling and greeting people with a handshake or a heartfelt hug. His parents hoped speech might return, but the medical staff told them his brain was too severely damaged, a common occurrence in survivors of lightning strikes near the head.

Years went by, and the family continued to visit our church on occasion. One Sunday when Lonnie was about twenty-four, he and his parents came for services. Lonnie walked up to the altar to greet me as I prepared for the next service to begin. I remembered I had wanted to ask if he'd had a near-death experience. I figured he could nod his head and answer yes-or-no questions. I told him about the "more than a hundred people" I'd talked to who had had the experience of seeing Jesus, angels, and dead relatives while clinically dead. I asked if this had happened to him. He was startled, his mouth fell open, and his eyes got very big, but at that moment his mother arrived to take him back to a pew.

"Lonnie," she said, "the service is about to start. We've got to go sit down."

Lonnie and I went our separate ways, but I was left with a partially answered question indicated by his reaction. Some months later, Lonnie and his family returned to the church. They sat in the front pew. Smiling, Lonnie jumped up and reached out to greet me.

"Hello, Father Price!" he said.

I staggered back in amazement! His mother grabbed me by the shoulders to explain that Lonnie started talking right after I'd asked him if he had had a near-death experience. She was stunned. Periodically he would tell her more of the experience, about how two angels and her deceased mother ("Your mom!") stood in the hospital room with him while he was recovering. He reported that his grandmother's spirit was in the intensive-care unit with them, and she would reach over and pat him on the face.

At one point, years before he recovered his speech, he saw a greeting card depicting two angels. He became happily agitated, making it clear that he wanted that card by clutching it to his chest. As his faltering speech returned, he explained that card depicted what he had seen in the hospital room: two angels standing by the bed. His mother acknowledged that she too had felt the presence of someone in the room, but never saw anyone.

It can be freeing, healing, and empowering to ask someone about the possibility of their having had this experience, giving them the opportunity to talk about a happening that could be thought odd, crazy, or simply a hallucination. But imagine the sheer joy Lonnie and his family must have felt when his speech returned, even though it is somewhat impaired. I urge you all, ask people who might have had a clinical death if they also had a near-death or after-death experience. The discussion that ensues can be immensely freeing. I wish I had asked Lonnie years earlier.

Stories like Lonnie's and Lou's underline the importance of sharing near-death accounts with as wide an audience as possible. In the past three years, three books—*The Boy Who Came Back from Heaven*, *Heaven Is for Real*, and *To Heaven and Back*[3]—have all resonated with mainstream America, bringing so much joy to readers around the country. This does not surprise me. Each one imparts wonderful—and consistent—details about heaven and describes in nearly identical language the overwhelming feeling of security, love, and peace each returnee experienced in God's presence. Individually, each book forces even the most skeptical reader to consider the fact that *something* does in fact happen when we die. The lights don't simply go out. Our stories continue. Collectively, these books—and the growing first-person accounts of near-death experiences—reveal that this *something* is bigger and more glorious than we ever dared to imagine.

# 10

# WHAT HEAVEN REVEALS

Those who return from heaven report an indescribably wonderful feeling of perfect love. There is no sexual component here, just a completely caring love that must be the purest *agapé* love. After all, Jesus didn't say to *like* your neighbor. We do not have to *like* our neighbors or approve of their lifestyle or idiosyncrasies, but we do have to *love* them.

John uses this word *agapé*—"love"—in his Gospel one hundred times, more than all the other three authors of the Gospels put together. Later, in his first letter, he wrote in Greek *theos agapé estin,* or "God is love" (1 John 4:8, 16). There is nothing ambiguous in the Greek or in the concept. Most returnees emphasize that very thing about God. Some report this was in stark contrast to what they had been taught about God's nature in their very strict religious communities.

Jeff, a water-well tech out in the Texas countryside, experienced this perfect love firsthand:

> I was bringing underground water to the surface. It was a good hard-core job. Out in the elements. Even in deep snow and big thunderstorms. Was at the job for a year now. Was a crazy job. Sometimes you had to lay down flat on your stomach 10 to 15 feet below ground to fish out the plumber's stub, so that you could make the connection to the well for water. Something you just don't think about when you're down there. You have to come to terms with your fears.
>
> In March I started to have these dreams for about a week. In these dreams I wasn't scared or afraid, but I was learning what to do when it caved in on me. By the end of the week I told it to stop. I never had them again and soon forgot about them.
>
> The next month my partner, Dale, and I headed to this commercial job out in the middle of nowhere. Was a deep well, 1800 feet or so. The trench was 2½ feet

across by 12 feet deep. Spring melting was going on, so the ground was heavy with water and the trench had about 6 feet of mud.

As I was looking over the job site to get a big picture, Dale was putting on the waders to run the copper line. He was just about to stand up when I insisted that I would run the copper line. After arguing a bit, he took them off. I slipped on the waders and headed down into the trench. I walked a quarter of it. It didn't feel right. Ground was shaking from the backhoe off in the distance. It was a deep one this time, and it was going to be a serious project. Dale went off to start on preparing the wellhead for the underground connection. As I was rolling out the big copper pipe, I'd step on it to keep it down in the muck.

After about 20 feet of this slow-going, bent-over muck job, something caught my eye. To my right the side of the trench was peeling away 6 feet above my head. This is where the dream kicked in. I let the pipe go and stood up against the opposite wall folding my arms across my chest. I yelled, "Dale!" and took a deep breath in and closed my eyes.

The ground had come over my head and pushed me down. A ton and a half of heavy ground was slowly crushing me to death. I asked myself, "Am I going to die?"

"Yes," someone said.

"There has to be another option here!"

"No," the voice replied.

Now I'm really being crushed to death. I scream in my head. The pain is way too much. I'm red-lining now. "When?!??" I scream in my head, as if it was going to be the last thought I ever have. There was a release from the body right at that moment. I was being pulled or carried out, and WE were moving fast. I thought, "What about my family?"

"They will be fine," the words vibrated my body. Whatever body I was in at that time. My eyes were still closed. No concern. No pain. Just total bliss.

I remember seeing my grandfather there. But I didn't remember him until years later when Grandma showed me a picture of him when he was young. I told her with tears in my eyes I had seen him.

There is much I still don't remember. But I remember seeing heaven from afar. It was like a city with a warm glow about it. Then in a flash, I'm in front of these great white stairs. I started to look up, not knowing where I am. As soon as I realized where I'm at, I hit the floor face down. Not feeling worthy of being there or this is my final judgment. I'm face down and in tears and very afraid and fearful.

Christ then picked me up and looked into me, then said, "I love you."

This too vibrated my whole being. I AM LOVE and JOY at this point. Next thing I know, I'm in a sphere. Peach colored, so it seemed. Being cradled by someone whom I just recently remembered because the Rev. [Bruce] Bonner had told me her name. I've been on this Wisdom search lately, and it all just started clicking together. I had seen her face in a slight awake dream state seven or eight years ago. My heart just ached for her. So beautiful. My heart just ached for her. I love her so, so much. Her name is Sophia ["wisdom," in Greek]. King Solomon talked about her. Now I know her too.

As I drifted to sleep in her arms, she slipped me back into my body. I felt something hit my head, and I opened my eyes. I was looking at Dale as he was digging me out. He was crying, and I can feel sorrow coming from him. I told him that I was fine and at peace. But he couldn't hear me. Why? I try to talk to him again. He's not listening. So I look over myself and realized that I wasn't breathing and that my whole body was shutting down. I could feel it. Like I was dying. I started to panic as I tried to remember what it felt like to breathe. "Breathe!" I say. . . . "Breathe. In, out, chest . . . damn . . . breathe."

Finally I took a breath like it was the first time. The pain hit me like a ton of bricks. Yeah. I'm back in my body now and I'm squished down to my knees. He just looked at me with those deer-in-the-headlight eyes. "Get me out of here!" I said. Just stares. Fine. I started to crawl out by myself holding my chest with one arm. I'm thinking I've got a broken rib, or a broken rib through the lung. I sit down at the top of the trench and whip the waders off. No cell phone at the time. No nearby pay phones. Darn, I think. No helicopter ride by Flight for Life. I'm thinking this qualified for that. So off we go for the hospital. Dale is driving like a madman, spilling equipment out of the back of the truck.

We arrived safely at the hospital emergency entrance. Dale is totally freaked out, while I was calm with peace, not knowing whether or not I was bleeding to death internally. I told him to just go in and get a wheelchair, because I didn't think I could walk

> anymore. Out come running two nurses and a doctor. They gently help me into the wheelchair and start heading to the emergency room. My clothes were off before they even got to the bed. At this point I don't remember much, because I was going in and out of consciousness. But I do remember my feet hanging off the end of the bed. The curtains were pulled around me, but opened at the foot of the bed with a 2-foot opening. My feet were so cold I remember. About then this beautiful, glowing nurse appears and touches both my feet, and this warmth comes over my entire body. Her smile and her eyes just penetrated my soul with love and reassurance.

Now, Jeff had not been baptized a Christian. Yet he and others like him with whom I've visited did not go to hell, but rather experienced God's wondrous love in heaven. How can we reconcile this with statements in the New Testament that say we must accept Jesus Christ as Lord and Savior in order to go to heaven?

I think the conclusion we can draw here is this. Jesus is, in Christian theology, God come to earth. Since God is love, so is Jesus, and he showed and commanded that love for us. Those who do live a life of love are, whether they know it or not, accepting Jesus in his command to love as the central orientation of their lives. Tragically, I know people who say they are Christians, but who do not lead loving, caring lives. When these mean-spirited people have near-death experiences, those experiences are often of the distressing or hellish kind.

## FEAR-BASED CHRISTIANITY

Garrison Keillor, in his *Prairie Home Companion* program on National Public Radio, talks humorously and pointedly about the "dark Lutherans" and "happy Lutherans" he grew up with nearby in Minnesota. Such a division is, of course, not limited to Lutherans, as we find the dark and the happy wings in all faith groups. I'm definitely in the "happy Lutherans" branch of the Episcopal Church. I do, however, know some dark Episcopalians.

Although they are somewhat simplified labels, "dark" and "happy" may be seen as representing the two ways religious congregations and their leaders go about the process of inserting their perception of God's will into religious practice. The former do so by frightening the faithful with hellfire and eternal damnation, with long lists of dos and don'ts to control unruly human wills. Many people are drawn to this approach, and some churches that proceed in this manner prosper and grow very strong.

I have heard that in some of her lectures Dr. Elisabeth Kübler-Ross related the story of a "hellfire and damnation" preacher who had a heart attack and died, but was resuscitated. As soon as he could, he got back into his pulpit and said, "Everything I've told you was wrong. God loves us and wants to forgive us. He loves, forgives, redeems." Kübler-Ross did not say what happened next. But, based on several instances I have heard of in which preachers changed their basic message from fear of God to God as love, I might hazard a guess that either the preacher was asked to leave or the congregation dwindled away.

Some preachers build a congregation based on fear of a wrathful, vindictive God who hates sinners. Within American Protestantism this tradition traces its lineage back to Jonathan Edwards during a period of American church history called the "Great Awakening," which occurred between 1730 and 1745. Edwards's 1741 sermon

"Sinners in the Hands of an Angry God" epitomizes the Puritan theology of this particular tradition down to this day.

"That was me," wrote Robert, the former fundamentalist pastor I mentioned earlier who had his own near-death experience and was annoyed that he had to return. "In fact, I used to tell people to read 'In the Hands of an Angry God'! I preached mean, angry. I made God out to be a being to be feared. All that foolishness." During Robert's near-death experience, he left his body and floated away:

> I went into what looked like a womb that was dark, except you could see in the dark. There was a yellow ball that lit up the womb, but even in the dark I could see. P. M. H. Atwater describes this exact scenario in one of her books. The dark place looks like a sonogram of a baby. Yet it's lit by the yellow light, but still was dark. Weird, I know. I believe I went into a womb of some nature to be healed. It was like my hard drive just got completely erased, and I came back to have to relearn.

He rested in this peaceful state for some time—"it seemed like five minutes"—and returned:

> The moment I woke up from the coma, I knew that I'd believed a lie that had hurt thousands of people. People would fill the churches up to hear this [lie]. I had a very charismatic personality. It seemed the less I preached in love, the more busy I stayed.

When he returned to his pulpit, he shared his new insight about a loving and forgiving God. The congregation melted away; his income went down to nothing. His family even turned away, except for his loving wife, who liked what he had become. I know of three preachers with similar backgrounds who lost their congregations when they switched to talk about a loving God.

Robert lost his career. He told me, "I can't tell those *lies* anymore. I can't preach that crap. I hurt thousands of people." He taught a religion of fear and now knows God offers a religion of love. I've had a great and challenging time sharing a loving version of Christianity with him. He is excited about learning to use God's love as a lens to see new insights in scripture. He now says, "Now that I *do* know the love of God and life, I have no place to share it. In my hospice work, I share my story with all my patients I think are open to it.

Never yet had one get offended when I tell them about going into the God of love."

Robert now knows God loves and forgives in every instance when one cries out to him. God gave another chance to the ones with whom I've spoken who were receiving hellish punishment when they cried out, "Lord, help me" or "Jesus, help me." God is not dogmatic or particular to a specific religion or sect. He is universal and, as John tells us, simply *love*. This revelation led Robert to quit his pastorate.

## OTHER RELIGIONS

In John 14:1–6 Jesus comforts his disciples by telling them:

> "Do not let your hearts be troubled. Believe in God, believe also in me. [2]In my Father's house there are many dwelling-places. If it were not so, would I have told you that I go to prepare a place for you? [3]And if I go and prepare a place for you, I will come again and will take you to myself, so that where I am, there

> you may be also. [4]And you know the way to the place where I am going." [5]Thomas said to him, "Lord, we do not know where you are going. How can we know the way?" [6]Jesus said to him, "I am the way, and the truth, and the life. No one comes to the Father except through me."

Christians take great comfort in this passage. It is commonly used in funeral services and in evangelical preaching about the need to "come to Jesus." As an Episcopal priest, I cannot argue with it except to point out that it seems to exclude non-Christians. How do I reconcile, then, this statement in the Gospel of John with the fact that I've read many near-death accounts similar to Christian ones by Muslims, Jews, Hindus, and an atheist? As well, I have talked to two Buddhists. Most of them do not include one factor, that of seeing Jesus, but often Christians do not report seeing Jesus either.

An answer more in keeping with what the thousands of positive, magnificent accounts relate would be that whoever lives lovingly is given the beautiful experience of being taken to heaven. And nine of the twelve people I talked to who did not have the beautiful experience had one thing in common: they lived their lives in a manner opposite of Jesus's commandment to "love one another as I have loved you."

God's love is not limited to Christians, but is for all people of goodwill who live with love for one another. The returnees show us this truth abundantly. I cannot in good conscience say that Christianity is the only way. I can say it is the way for me. I can say God's love is not exclusive to Christianity or Judaism or Islam or Hinduism or Buddhism or any other faith group, since members of each group embrace and live the command that we are to love one another.

There are people in every group who preach and live hate. Watch the evening news to find them killing others for not being "pure." Pray for them, that God will heal them in whatever way God knows they need. God's love pervades the lives of people of all faiths. Jesus said, "I have other sheep that do not belong to this fold. I must bring them also, and they will listen to my voice. So there will be one flock, one shepherd" (John 10:16). His voice of love is heard all over the planet.

## DOCTRINE VERSUS EXPERIENCE

My experience with other returnees tells me it may take many years for them to sort out what their near-death experience means for them. When Paul in 2 Corinthians 12:2 talks about a man who "fourteen years ago" went to the "third heaven," those fourteen years may well indicate how long it took Paul to decide to talk about his experience. Jeff waited nearly twenty years before he called me to talk about his near-death experience. I'm hoping that others like Robert will be able to find an understanding person to be involved in their spiritual recovery, so that it won't take that long for them. In Robert's case, think of the work to be done in dealing with the contrast between such a loving experience and what he had been believing and teaching all his adult life about God.

Some Christians seriously denigrate these accounts, since they present a very different concept of God, Jesus, sin, the role of the cross, redemption, and salvation than what they have been taught or teach. When God is seen as remote, wrathful, and vengeful, it's hard to accept firsthand accounts of the intangible spirit world as loving and forgiving. As a result, returnees, armed with new insights about God and religion, often feel alienated and confused around other congregants or family and friends who insist on believing their preconceived notions about God.

In *Evidence of the Afterlife: The Science of Near-Death Experiences,* Jeff Long reports it is quite common for returnees to drop out of church participation if they belong to a church where rigidity and "shall nots" run counter to their new knowledge of God's unconditional love and forgiveness.[1] Those who have just gone through the review of their life with Jesus now know firsthand the areas of their lives that need restoration. They know that God is a God of love and redemption from guilt and remorse. This amazing *love* is a key component bringing about change in the lives of so many experiencers. The result is a far more empathetic person.

Some Christian groups (the Roman Catholic Church is only the largest, most vocal example) teach that sex is reserved for the purpose of procreation and to subvert that process is a serious sin. Thus, birth control, abortion, and masturbation are declared to be serious sins and homosexual acts a grave disorder of natural law, all subject to excommunication and eternal punishment. Psychiatrists maintain that some 95 percent of people masturbate, but less than 6 percent of the returnees with whom I've spoken had distressing or hellish experiences. Those distressing events resulted from the habitually more or less unloving lives of nine of the twelve. Furthermore, the three homosexuals with whom I discussed heaven have reported it as a beautiful experience. They did not face condemnation or damnation. Nine of the twelve people with whom I've spoken who had either distressing or hellish experiences were simply mean-spirited or cruel people. And some of them had been active members of various churches, including the ones I served.

Many cultural taboos, which perhaps made sense at one time in some places, have been made into religious dogma for all time and have robbed people of what would have been an authentic life for them. Sometimes cultural taboos are made into religious dogma, which then are made into law. The British and American missionaries who evangelized Africa in the nineteenth century established a mind-set that led some African nations to declare that homosexuals should be punished by death. All of which gives extra weight to Jesus's several admonitions that we are not to judge, lest we be judged ourselves (e.g., Matthew 7:1).

No returnees report "thousands of years in purgatory." If there is a purgatory, it is simply the brief, *lovingly conducted* life review during which the deceased sees all the good—and bad—he or she has done and feels the happiness—and hurt—caused others. Many thousands of near-death accounts recall this. Although recitations of the Lord's Prayer or the Hail Mary and the giving of money are indeed worthwhile spiritual disciplines, they are not primary in the life review—being a loving person is. Anyone can recite or perform religious acts of devotion and then turn right around and act unlovingly toward others, the antithesis of the Lord's new commandment. Isaiah and Amos both prophesied against otherwise worthwhile acts of worship not accompanied by righteous living. Amos said, on behalf of the Lord, "I hate, I despise your festivals, and I take no delight in your solemn assemblies. . . . But let justice roll down like waters, and righteousness like an ever-flowing stream" (5:21, 24).

The review of one's life in the near-death experiences shows that long lists of mortal and venial sins are not particularly relevant to going to heaven. There is one "mortal" sin that will result in a distressing experience—that of living unlovingly. The many with whom I've visited relate this insight.

Many denominational positions on who goes to hell and why are overturned. One stance on the subject is that a finite number of people are going to heaven: "one hundred forty-four thousand" (Revelation 7:4). This is a misunderstanding of the statement, which lists twelve thousand from each of the twelve tribes "of Israel" who were sealed by the angel. As well, a significant number of conservative Christians of various denominations, even some of my own Episcopalians, believe strongly that no one goes to heaven until Jesus returns and lifts the righteous ones out of the graves. The thousands of accounts of returnees refute both beliefs.

After his near-death experience, Jeff went to see his pastor. "You couldn't have gone to heaven," his pastor told him. "You haven't been baptized yet. And we don't go to heaven until Jesus comes back and lifts us out of the grave." But Jeff's story showed that Christian baptism is not required to enter heaven. Unbaptized children do not go to "limbo" when they die, Little Fran and Colton Burpo tell us. They go to the arms of Jesus. In Luke 23:43, Jesus promises "Paradise . . . today" to the *unbaptized* but repentant thief on the cross next to him. Clearly, the thousands of near-death accounts show there is no waiting for Jesus to return. In many accounts, Jesus's return was at the moment the person passed into the next life.

Baptism is a sacrament. The act is the outward and visible sign of an inward and spiritual grace, the absolution of one's sins so that one is able to enter heaven. But baptism is just that—a symbol, a sacrament, an initiation into the institutional church. The cleansing of sin is done not by the earthly action of sprinkling, dunking, immersing, or spraying, but by solely God's grace.

## THE PRIMACY OF LOVE

The reports from those who went through the review of their lives and reaffirm what God was concerned about reflect Jesus's new commandment: "Love one another as I have loved you." Any actions counter to this directive come under enlightened criticism and then are forgiven. People who live lives utterly counter to this command report distressing or hellish experiences, depending upon the severity and extent of their unloving actions.

Ethics addresses the question of how we shall conduct our lives, make our decisions, and plan our paths. Ethics, as demonstrated by the review of the lives of the returnees, shows selfless love, *agapé* love, as directed by Jesus and extolled by Paul to be the basis for our lives. How shall we live? Lovingly. What can we do for our fellow human beings, indeed, for all creation? Love them as fellow children of God, which they are.

Of utmost importance is what John said in his first letter: "God is love" (4:8, 16). It is what Paul said in 1 Corinthians 13 about the primacy of *agapé* love in our lives. It is what Jesus meant when he commanded, "Love one another as I have loved you" (John 15:12). It is what he meant in the parable of the good Samaritan when he led the lawyers to understand what it means to "love your neighbor" and how central that is to the Christian life (Luke 10:25–37).

Rob Bell's statements about heaven and hell in *Love Wins* reflect what I observe from accounts of near-death experiences and have since come to understand about God.[2] God's love for us is so complete that he came among us to show us how *agapé* love works in human lives. That love so confronts the human establishment in any age that it brings about repression and aggression against the messenger. The prophets were routinely killed for their efforts. For Jesus, in the age in which he came, that inevitably produced death on a cross. God's power was revealed through Jesus's death and subsequent resurrection. He then spent more time with his disciples to show them what they could not understand until their preconceived notions died on the cross with him.

God's love is more powerful than death and overcomes it. This was a foregone conclusion from the beginning, the creation of the universe. The continuing life about which the returnees tell us is the truth about life and death: it is all a gift from God out of his abundant love for his creation.

God is ultimately concerned about the way we live our lives while on earth. We are to share God's love, share the gifts God gives us, knowing we create our own heaven or hell here for others and ourselves while we are alive. Those who have experienced the life review report God's one commandment is to live in love.

# CONCLUSION

Near-death experiences open an astonishing window into the nature and will of God—and into heaven and hell. From them, we learn deep insights into what happens after death, life's greatest mystery. Through that window comes a clarifying light onto our life here and now in so many areas. The returnees uniformly say human language cannot adequately express what they experienced: the overwhelming love, the magnificent beauty, the overpowering joy—and peace. Our superlatives are inadequate to describe the reality, nature, and quality of life that awaits us all at death. This is one reason returnees may take many years to sort out, discuss, and share what happened in heaven.

I was stunned when I first encountered two powerful near-death experiences. Suddenly it was clear that all my assumptions about life after death were, at best, incomplete. At worst, they were occasionally contrary to what Christianity teaches, that Christ died that we might have eternal life. Raymond Moody and Private Alberto opened my mind to the reality of the loving, beautiful, and joyful nature of eternal life in heaven after death. Near-death experiences show us that God actually *is,* that God is loving, understanding, and forgiving. We learn from the returnees that errors we make in life through sin are forgivable even after death. We need only ask and accept the forgiveness and the eternal life God offers us.

Christian theology teaches that God came to earth in the form of an infant with a plan for our life, here and hereafter. Through his birth, life, death, resurrection, and ascension to the right hand of God the Father, he shows us the place of God's love in our life. An angel relayed to Mary, his mother, and Joseph, his foster father, that this child was to be given the name Y'shua. Translated into English and Spanish, we know the name as "Jesus." The Hebrew name means "God saves."

So the earthly ministry of Jesus accomplished two things. First, in his life and ministry he embodied the *agapé* nature of God; his very presence taught us how to live. Jesus's loving nature confronted earthly powers, which are always corrupted to some degree by human sin. That confrontation drove the authorities to kill him. Second, God overcame death with the resurrection of Jesus's body. He was assumed bodily into heaven, where he sits at the right hand of God the Father and Creator. Two returnees reported seeing and interacting with Jesus, who was sitting at the right side of God the Father.

It needs to be said that Christianity does not have three gods. We see God acting in three distinct roles: as Creator, described as Father; as Redeemer, called Jesus; and as continuing Spirit, called the Holy Spirit. G. Ernest Wright spelled out this explanation of the doctrine of the Trinity in his book *God Who Acts,* defining the Trinity by the function of each person of the three.[1] His was the most helpful work for me on this complicated and important doctrine. It can be easily demonstrated even in the Hebrew scriptures (the Tanakh), which Christians call the Old Testament. The Judeo-Christian-Islamic creation story is told in Genesis 1–2. In Genesis 1:1, "In the beginning . . . God created the heavens and the earth," we see the Creator at work. Job made the bold statement of faith: "I know that my Redeemer lives, and that at the last he will stand upon the earth; . . . then in my flesh I shall see God, whom I shall see on my side, and my eyes shall behold, and not another" (19:25–27). Here we see the second person of the Trinity, later to be named Y'shua, Jesus, "God saves." And in Genesis 1:2 (NIV), "The Spirit of God was hovering over the waters." In this, we see the Holy Spirit present at creation.

Jews, Christians, and Muslims know from our common Abrahamic faith that God loves us. Scripture supports this fact, as does the witness of thousands who have returned from heaven. Returnees reiterate that God's love for us is far deeper than any theologian can fathom. From that love comes his understanding of us, which is far deeper than all the psychologists, psychiatrists, or philosophers can comprehend. From that understanding comes his forgiveness of us, more thorough than any clergy can grasp. From that forgiveness comes complete redemption for service in his kingdom. And from that love comes salvation for eternal life. Redemption is for this life; salvation is for the next, eternal life.

Robert, the former hellfire-and-damnation preacher, preached like Jeremiah for thirty years, full of wrath and woe, on radio stations across the South. Thousands attended his services. He told me the more hate he preached, the more people flocked to his church. Then he had his near-death experience, and it turned his understanding around.

One insight that I shared with him stunned him the most. It comes from John 11, in which Jesus visited Mary and Martha four days after the death of their brother, Lazarus. In that story is the famous shortest verse in the Bible—"Jesus wept." The Gospel account relates that the Jews standing by said, "See how he loved him!" (11:35, 36, NIV). Then Jesus raised Lazarus from the dead.

I don't think the Jews understood why Jesus wept. I think he wept because he knew he was going to have to bring his friend back to life—from Paradise! Robert explained to me that this is exactly how he feels—he wishes he could have stayed in heaven! If you'd had four days in Paradise, would you want to have to come back to this world? Many returnees are not happy with God for sending them back and angry with the medics who brought them back to life.

I find there are really only two religions in the world: a religion of love and a religion of fear. This understanding cuts across all major faith groups. We see saints and ordinary loving people as well as vicious, radical people in each group. Those who have been to heaven and returned testify repeatedly and uniformly to the validity in God's eyes of the loving approach to life. The beautiful experience occurs for those who live their lives in love, as Jesus commanded.

The insights from these accounts speak to us emphatically about God's loving nature and command to us to love. That is how we are to live, in love, together. All the life reviews assure us that God is with us even in our worst moments. God suffers along with the victims, knowing how badly people treat one another. From the annals of the near-death experiences, we know God loves, forgives, and redeems all people when they ask. As well, God lovingly brings us on into heaven for the continuing journey of our lives. The accounts of the near-death experiences need to be shouted from the rooftops, as they tell us such profound truths.

# ACKNOWLEDGMENTS

During my years as a chaplain at St. Luke's Episcopal Hospital in the Texas Medical Center in Houston, Texas, I did benefit from and greatly appreciate the early support I received from Reynolds Delgado, M.D., cardiologist and colleague. His was the strongest voice of the medical staff urging me to write about the accounts being shared. Many people had told me I should "write a book." I regularly replied that there were enough books out there by people who'd had the experience. As well, there were several books by M.D.'s who had researched the subject and written up their conclusions. I am in neither category.

What finally made the most sense came from one friend at Palmer Memorial Episcopal Church, Cameron Payne. He pointed out that as a pastor I saw the many implications from an extraordinary number of accounts related to me by people who have had a variety of experiences and should share these insights.

I have received great support and advice from Jody Long, J.D., and Jeffrey Long, M.D. They established the Near-Death Experience Research Foundation in 1998. They not only helped me with some serious questions I had, but they invited me to post some of my pastoral experiences on their website. After adding my contact data to their website, many more people contacted me telling of their experiences and asking questions.

Thanks must go to Palmer Memorial Episcopal Church, Houston, Texas, the Rector, the Rev. James W. Nutter, his staff, and many members. They encouraged me and gave me a large venue in which to work on the concept. In fact, it was after I gave a lecture to a large Sunday crowd on the subject that Cameron Payne made the breakthrough point for me that gave me the vision for this book: explore the meanings and implications of the accounts.

I am deeply grateful to Anne Grizzle for introducing me to Harper's editors and to the HarperOne staff for all their support, encouragement, and hard work on this book.

# Acknowledgments

I am deeply grateful to my wife, Arlene, for encouraging me, helping me write, organize, and edit a mass of details and reflections, insights, and contacts. I was told by someone who read the manuscript, "you're a very good writer." I replied, "My wife and I are a good writing team." And it is true. I write; she organizes and edits.

# NOTES

CHAPTER 1: ALBERTO'S STORY

1. Raymond A. Moody Jr., *Life After Life* (Atlanta, GA: Mockingbird Books, 1975).

CHAPTER 3: IT'S IN THE BIBLE

1. Jaime Clark-Soles, *Death and the Afterlife in the New Testament* (New York: T&T Clark, 2006), p. 13.
2. Bernard W. Anderson, *Understanding the Old Testament* (Englewood Cliffs, NJ: Prentice Hall, 1957), pp. 512–16.
3. Kenneth Barker, ed., *The NIV Study Bible* (Grand Rapids, MI: Zondervan, 1995), p. 1431. William Baird, "Commentary on the Gospel According to Luke," in *The Interpreter's One-Volume Commentary on the Bible,* ed. Charles M. Laymon (Nashville, TN: Abingdon, 1971), p. 672.
4. Frederick C. Grant, "Commentary on Mark," in *The Interpreter's Bible,* vol. 7 (Nashville, TN: Abingdon, 1951), p. 886.
5. Donald Guthrie, "2 Corinthians," in *Eerdmans' Handbook to the Bible,* eds. David Alexander et al. (Tring, Herts, England: Lion, 1973), p. 600.
6. James L. Price, "Commentary on the Second Letter of Paul to the Corinthians," in *Interpreter's One-Volume Commentary on the Bible,* ed. Charles M. Laymon, p. 822.

CHAPTER 4: A HISTORY OF NEAR-DEATH EXPERIENCES

1. Carl Jung, *Memories, Dreams, and Reflections* (New York: Vintage Books, 1989), p. 291.
2. Kenneth Ring, *Life at Death* (New York: Coward, McCann, & Geoghegan, 1980).
3. George Gallup Jr. and William Proctor, *Adventures in Immortality* (New York: McGraw-Hill, 1982), pp. 200–201.
4. www.Ballparksofbaseball.com/1980-89attendance.htm.

CHAPTER 5: MY STORY CONTINUED

1. Liz Dale, *Crossing Over and Coming Home* (Houston, TX: Emerald Ink, 2008).

CHAPTER 6: HOW DEATH WORKS

1. "The Memorial Service for Steve Jobs," *New York Times Online*, Monday, October 30, 2011.
2. Carla Wills-Brandon, *One Last Hug Before I Go: The Mystery and Meaning of Deathbed Visions* (Deerfield Beach, FL: Health Communications, Inc., 2000), pp. 171–72.
3. Raymond A. Moody Jr., *Glimpses of Eternity: Sharing a Loved One's Passage from This Life to the Next* (New York: Guideposts, 2010).
4. Pim van Lommel, "Near-Death Experience in Survivors of Cardiac Arrest," in *Lancet*, 2001; 358: 2039–45.
5. Kenneth Ring and Sharon Cooper, *Mindsight: Near-Death and Out-of-Body Experiences in the Blind* (New York: iUniverse, 2008).
6. George Ritchie, *Return from Tomorrow* (Chicago: Chosen Press, 1978), pp. 44–46.

CHAPTER 7: HOW HEAVEN WORKS

1. Mary C. Neal, *To Heaven and Back* (Colorado Springs: WaterBrook, 2012).
2. Todd Burpo, *Heaven Is for Real* (Nashville, TN: Nelson, 2010), p. 159.
3. Burpo, *Heaven Is for Real*, pp. 86–88.
4. Howard Storm, *My Descent into Death* (New York: Doubleday, 2005), p. 38.

## CHAPTER 9: THE RETURN

1. Anita Moorjani, *Dying to Be Me: My Journey from Cancer, to Near Death, to True Healing* (Carlsbad, CA: Hay House, 2012).
2. Don Piper, *Ninety Minutes in Heaven* (Grand Rapids, MI: Revell, 2004).
3. Kevin Malarkey, *The Boy Who Came Back from Heaven* (Carol Stream, IL: Tyndale, 2010); Burpo, *Heaven Is for Real;* Mary C. Neal, *To Heaven and Back.*

## CHAPTER 10: WHAT HEAVEN REVEALS

1. Jeffrey Long, *Evidence of the Afterlife: The Science of Near-Death Experiences* (San Francisco: HarperOne, 2010).
2. Rob Bell, *Love Wins* (San Francisco: HarperOne, 2011).

## CONCLUSION

1. G. Ernest Wright, *God Who Acts* (London: SCM, 1960).